The Keeper

Notes of Amazing Love

IRMA FLANAGAN

WESTBOW
PRESS®
A DIVISION OF THOMAS NELSON
& ZONDERVAN

WestBow Press books may be ordered through booksellers or by contacting:

WestBow Press
A Division of Thomas Nelson & Zondervan
1663 Liberty Drive
Bloomington, IN 47403
www.westbowpress.com
1 (866) 928-1240

Scripture taken from the New King James Version®. Copyright © 1982 by Thomas Nelson. Used by permission. All rights reserved.

Scripture taken from the King James Version of the Bible.

ISBN: 978-1-9736-1135-6 (sc)
ISBN: 978-1-9736-1134-9 (hc)
ISBN: 978-1-9736-1136-3 (e)

Library of Congress Control Number: 2017919193

Print information available on the last page.

WestBow Press rev. date: 01/16/2018

I am continually amazed at the wonders and grace of the great Keeper of our souls. With one touch, a troubled heart is at peace; with one whisper, a life has meaning; with one vision, the wonders of heaven are opened.

We have but to look out the window to see a cardinal sitting in a rhododendron bush or a deer eating leaves from the trees to see the works of His hands. We may walk in California's Redwood Forest or among giant sequoias, stand on the slope of Mount Washburn with its acres upon acres of blooming flowers, gaze at the mighty expanse of the Grand Canyon or the mountains and lakes of the Southern Appalachians—and be awed by His creation.

Yet many of us are filled with constant struggle, upheaval, and turmoil. Without the awareness of God's presence, we feel as if we are free falling with no bungee cord attached protecting us from hitting the ground, though the winds and the cord's resistance bob us up and down.

Regardless of one's age, ethnicity, or economic status, beginning the day with a reminder of God's eternal love changes attitudes, and thus, opens hearts and minds to experiences of happiness, peace, and accomplishment. Though this book is in no way intended to be a substitute for reading the Bible, my prayer is that these writings will point readers to God's word and to Him who created and loves them and who holds the unshifting truth of their identity and purpose.

I am indebted to my parents and family, who were and are godly people, to my church family, many of whom I have known and loved for a lifetime, and to friends like Colleen Swanson and Diane Hale, who have inspired me to draw ever closer to the Lord. The writing groups in Jasper, Hiawassee, and Blairsville have been a tremendous support and I am grateful to Elizabeth Dyer for her constant computer assistance. I also appreciate my Facebook and email friends who have read my devotionals and encouraged me to continue writing.

Lost Lamb

Its breath faint, its eyes weak, its wool scraggly and dirty, the lamb lay on His shoulder. His head leaned toward it, His hand lovingly rubbing its head, neck, and body. The shepherd had found it in the thistles, lost and lifeless. The thief in the form of wanderer's lust had stolen it away, led it farther into the wilderness, and made sure it lost its way.

In such a condition, the Lord found us, restored us, and gave us new life. The blossoming desert yet entices us occasionally, and we respond to its deceptive allure. The flowers that blanket the hillside are temporary and fragile, and the flowers that we tucked in our hair yesterday are wilted today. When we are in such a condition, our Savior hears our desperate cries for restoration, finds us, wipes away our hurt, and brings us back to His gracious joy-filled land. The friendship that had been tried is restored; the home that had been rejected is offered and claimed once again; and the tasteless food has become tasty again, for the Lord has restored the savor of its saltiness. "Return to me and I will return to you," He says.

Isaiah 35:1
Zechariah 1:3
Luke 14:34, 15:5

How precious you are to God! Gold refined in the fire so that it is devoid of impurities is not as valuable in God's eyes as you are. Gold and diamonds possess flaws. The Smithsonian's prized Hope Diamond, valued at over $200 million, has trace amounts of boron atoms that give it its blue color. The Savior who died for you had no such impurity. God, who wants His creation to be holy and pure as He is holy, must have felt brokenhearted as He saw Adam and Eve make a decision that led them and humankind to a wilderness of barrenness and trouble. Evidencing a contrasting view, Peter told the lame man that he did not have silver and gold. What he had was more precious, because faith is the substance of God. It is the hint, the faint aroma, the savory morsel of things to come. Whereas metals are extraneous materials subject to being lost, God's love dwells within. Never will it be lost. Never will it fail. Never will you find a disillusioning impurity. His love for you has been refined in the fire. It is without spot or blemish.

1 Peter 1:7, 17–19
Acts 3:6

You are not alone. Wherever you go physically, mentally, socially, or emotionally, our Lord has been there before you. Not only has He gone before you, but the Holy Spirit is always with you. Isaiah says that the glory of the Lord is the rearguard of the righteous. He is the protector at the place where you are most frequently attacked—that place where you're not looking nor about which you are thinking. When Elisha's servant feared the attack of the Syrians, God opened his eyes so that he could see the angel army with its thousands of chariots on the hillside. When Peter was bound with two chains and sleeping between two guards in prison, an angel delivered him. David says the angel of the Lord encamps around those who respect and fear the Lord. Though lions may go hungry, those who love and seek the Lord will not lack any good thing. The ever-present shepherd abides with us and keeps us on the straight and safe path. Our deliverer, who has the resources of heaven at His disposal, never fails.

Psalm 34:7, 10
Isaiah 52:12, 58:8
2 Kings 6:17
Acts 12:6

The cloudy morning brings a coolness to the walk across Lake Chatuge Dam. To the left, green tree-covered islands break the water as it reflects the cloud-piercing light. The peaceful scene is a reminder that He who holds back the floodwaters of life walks with us in peace. What a powerful yet gentle Savior. He who has the power to build and destroy nations is He whose hand gently wipes the tears from our eyes. The deceit and evil of the kingdoms of Isaiah's and Daniel's day were no match for the Son of Man. His whisper says to His faithful, "The song of the terrible one will be diminished." The veil of death "that is spread over the nations" will be destroyed.

The same Lord who has power over the world brings peace to the heart. His steadfast love does not change whether we are talking about the general or the specific, for His nature does not change. He is who He is, and He is a totally present God. Isaiah says, "We have waited for Him, and He will save us." The Word itself, the Word who is the Lord, has spoken. He sees you. Feel His gentle hand as He wipes away the worry and stress from your heart. Hear Him say, "You 'shall walk with me in white ...' beyond the struggles of the world."

Isaiah 25:5–9
John 1:1
Daniel 7:24–27
Revelation 3:4

Constancy

The vines hanging heavy with grapes greet the dew-receding day with peace. The fruit radiates confidence that the provision for tomorrow has been made; the food is available to be preserved. How gracious God has been. He who keeps the vineyard has "[watered] it every moment … has [kept] it night and day." Constancy is His nature, consistent nurturing His promise. He who died for His vineyard will not leave, or neglect, or ignore. He gives the quietness and confidence that is our strength. Anxious haste does not speed God's design, for He is the master controller, intentional and wise. Having been eyewitnesses of His power and having felt Holy Spirit flowing through our branches, we rest in the keeper of the vine. His all-seeing eye sees our needs, our desires, and our hopes as He shapes the roots, the vines, the leaves, and the grapes with attention to every detail of light and darkness. The color comes; our lives are renewed. We see that His wise husbandry is beyond reproach, and we trust His love.

Isaiah 27:3, 30:15

Are you prepared to receive God's blessings—the revelations of His great love for you? His attentions are turned toward you as you go about your business. You can trust in the whisper of His voice that tells you to gather the vessels or to sow the seeds. Though your life may abound in physical gifts, His great gift is the gift of sight, for He is the light that demolishes darkness. As He gave the blind beggar the ability to see at the pool of Siloam, He also gave him the knowledge of Himself as the "sent one" of God. Imagine the man's awe as he saw the wondrous works of God for the first time: the water in the pool, the curvatures of his fingers, the sun breaking through the clouds, and the face of a friend. Surely, he remembered how his vision became clearer with each step as he returned from the pool to see the physical face of Jesus. How glad he must have been that he obeyed the Lord who said, "Go, wash." Faith turns our eyes toward Him, seeking to know His instruction. Preparing means trusting enough to act upon what He says. Take time to bask in the light of His love today.

Job 37:14
John 9:5–7

The long, soft cooing of the dove could be heard along the gently flowing waters of the Jordan River as it flowed into the peaceful Sea of Galilee. It was an important day—the day the Holy Spirit would identify the Christ. As John lifted Jesus from the water, "He saw the Spirit of God descending like a dove." The Spirit's appearing like a dove must have assured Jesus, who recognized its elusive, peace-loving nature, its plump, well-fed body, and its silver underwings and the gold of its neck.

It is the elusive that fascinates us the most—that ethereal suggestion of the more that we cannot grasp exactly. However, like Noah who saw that the dove had returned to feed its young the green leaves and knew land had been found, we know the reality of a place in the distance. The sensitive, nurturing Holy Spirit—like the dove, the bird most worthy of sacrifice because of its loving, peaceful qualities—had identified the Savior of the world. The sweet, cooing peace of the Holy Spirit still identifies that which is of the Spirit within us today. It is the peace that goes with us into the wilderness as it did with Jesus immediately after His baptism. It is the peace in the storm. We listen for His sweet voice.

Matthew 3:16–18, 4:1–11
Genesis 6–9

Friends

Brothers and sisters are special beings who love and laugh, fight and scratch, hold grudges and hopefully forgive, and love and laugh together again. How true is the Proverb that says, "As man sharpens iron, so a man sharpens the countenance of his friend"! Life is more exciting, and we grow through our interactions with each other. Expressing thoughts or ideas so we get others' reactions helps us refine and clarify our own. Hmm … how surprising to think that our siblings and friends help us to become smarter!

The Lord desires that His children have that feeling of kinship. Jesus, our elder brother, spent His life on earth bringing provision and nourishment for us, His siblings. He said that no one has greater love than someone who "lays down his life" for his friends, which is what brothers and sisters often become. The best relationships are those that involve both give and take. Jesus gave His life for us. When we accept Him as our Savior, we give ours for Him—and what an honor it is to do so. Then, how special are subsequent friendships of brothers and sisters in Christ!

Proverbs 27:17
John 15:13

We need see only a person's hands and we know his or her gender, age, and often general occupation. We remember the hands of our mothers, fathers, children, friends, and mentors. Hands are the tools of activity and accomplishment. Psalm 90 relates the work of our hands to the beauty of God: "and let the beauty of the Lord our God be upon us, and establish the work of our hands." To use our hands for the work God has put before us is indeed a beautiful thing. Hands guide us in the love of the Lord. The hands of angels "bear you up, lest you dash your foot against a stone." Their touch is our comfort when we are "on your (our) knees and on the palms of your (our) hands" as was Daniel when the hands of Michael, the archangel, touched him. Michael said, "I have been sent to you … for from the first day that you set your heart to understand and to humble yourself before God, your words were heard; and I have come because of your words." The hands of the Master hold you close and hug you tightly in His love.

Deuteronomy 7:7, 10:15
Daniel 10:11–14
Psalm 90:17, 91:12–16

Surrounded by Love

Can you see yourself basking in the reality of God's affection for you? John says that heaven's streets are paved with gold, that the walls of the New Jerusalem are made of jasper and the gates are made of pearl. How beautiful! Yet, what a metaphor I see, describing the extreme love our Lord has for us! Heaven's gates are the open arms of God, like the father's open arms who welcomed home his prodigal son. The walls of jasper and streets of gold are the fatted calf of God's love for His children. Every item speaks of love. No pearl compares to the beauty of acceptance into the innermost heart of the loving master whose intent is pure, whose loving hands have cleansed us with the precision and attention of the ultimate jeweler, whose grace has returned us to the fulfilled, happy state we traded for knowledge of good and evil in the garden of Eden.

Revelation 21:21
Luke 15:11–32

The Hand of God

How far does the hand of God reach? The hand that holds us senses our every thought, desire, and emotion. We cannot count His thoughts toward us, for they are continual and extensive. Where can we hide from God? The privacy we have from other people does not include God. His love for us means that His thoughts are not condemning, but protective, His desire for us being regenerating life and growth.

Can we run from Him? Why would we try? He who made us "fearfully and wonderfully," and who knows our every cell, will turn the darkness into light so that He may find His child, to give him the best. David says, "If I ascend into heaven, you are there; If I make my bed in hell, behold You are there." The God who knows our dreams and the motivations of our hearts, and who fashioned our days, sees our substance. The intimacy of God's amazing love provides the foundation for the good things of life and spirit. Praise God for His love!

Psalm 139

Is that you I hear singing? The noise of rejoicing, your sounds of joyful praise, reflects your strength as the joy of the Lord reigns. What do we have to be so happy about? Toward the end of King David's life, when he was old and feeble, his son Adonijah began to reign without David's knowledge. When David became aware of it, he called Zadok the priest to anoint the chosen king, Solomon. In Gihon beside the river that flows out of Eden, Solomon was anointed king while Adonijah sought to hold on to the horns of the altar. Solomon spared his life.

Today we rejoice because God has "anointed Jesus of Nazareth with the Holy Ghost and with power," and He has spared our lives. Today He reigns. Today we hold to the horns of the altar and the mercy of Jesus Christ. Do you hear His laughter, His joy, because you depend upon His power and love? Your voice of praise is beautiful. Don't stop singing.

Acts 10:38
Nehemiah 8:9
1 Kings 1:15–53

Is the water frozen? A day such as this one, when ice hangs from the roof and the driveway is slippery, is perfect for hibernation—a free day to just rest or play games. Hopefully, the water is not frozen inside, for it is the Spirit of the Lord that brings release from the concerns of the mind and heart, that enables you to build a spiritual house within, and that gives you power to move forward in victory. Your spirit is released by God's Spirit that unfetters, that brings joy, that brings life. Sometimes living water flows like Niagara Falls, giving you power to do amazing things. Sometimes it is graceful, like Yosemite's falling waters, healing the spot that is sore, reminding you of His love, bringing you to a place of rest. Sometimes it is a trickle, like a slowly growing stream. Bringing yourself into a mental stance of humility and worship touches God and opens His reservoir. May yours be a day of free-flowing water.

Zechariah 4:6

The Love that Gives

Little children, do you remember the free days of childhood, the sense of wonder you felt, the sense of security, the warmth of parental or familial love, the feeling of acceptance? How nice were the products of that love: the dolls, the toy cars, the balls, and the games! One day, without realizing it, we began focusing on the material things. The school environment took us into having what others have—the right backpack, the right toys, the right clothes, the right friends, the right car. Chains began to lock us to the "we-have-to-haves." We became willing to work for them, willing to spend all our waking hours for them.

One day we, like the prodigal son, realized that it's all superficial, unnecessary, even shallow. "What manner of love" the Father has for us that we can go home to a greater joy than even that which we knew as little children, that keys of love can unlock the chains, that canons of life-giving water can break down the walls of appearance and longing, that the enduring care of the heavenly Father stands ever ready to give us the spiritual gifts our earthly father cannot. We find that it's about the love that gives rather than the materials themselves.

1 John 2:1, 3:1
Luke 15:11–32

The time has come to break free of the worries that tie you down and take away your life, the ones that have come one by one like little threads that tie a cloth. They keep you from living in the moment, causing you to miss the fullness of life. God holds the future as He does today. Jesus came "to give light to those in darkness" and that we "should be saved from our enemies." Unwarranted concern about things you cannot control is an evil warrior that seeks to steal your life, to put you in a dark dungeon where you are bound by chains.

As the poets say, "Seize the day," focusing on the positive traits in the people, situations, and things around you. They are here but for a time, as are you. Live while you are living. It is not how perfect the situation, but how you value the perfections in it, not how valuable a thing is, but the richness you see in it. The overall wealth you hold is in the trust that God guides your path, that He holds your todays and your tomorrows. You can enjoy the good things of the present. Live in the joys of the day God has given you.

Luke 1:71, 79

God's Bakery

Millstones are circular rocks whose purpose is to grind grain. Their whirring is a pleasant sound, one that promises food and nourishment to come. God does not want you to feel burdened, as if a millstone were hanging from your neck. Hung from the neck, the weight is unbearable, and you drown in your troubles. Burdens come in many forms: a job you do not want to do, a feeling of guilt, someone who irritates you, unforgiveness, worry.

When your cares are given to the Lord as He says you are to do, the heavy weight becomes easy; the millstone becomes a flat pebble fit for skipping across the water. When you look forward with hope and trust in the Lord who cares for you, the millstone does not foreshadow doom but God's nourishment. May you smell the savory, alluring odor of God's bakery today.

Matthew 6:27
Jeremiah 25:10

What has the power to make you smile? Physicists define power as "the amount of energy produced in a given amount of time." It is important to us who love light. Smiles are usually immediate, a burst of energy. Like springtime, which seems to burst forth effortlessly, the love of God produces surges of energy within and over us. It comes in the ray of hope, the energy of joy, the touch of healing. With Jesus, power focused itself in calming the wind and waves, in healing the sick, in multiplying the loaves and fishes, in teaching truth, in forgiving, in igniting a love of life within us, in enabling us who are weak. The master of power in every form is our God. His is the power of gentleness, of might, of creativity, of love, of integrity, of truth, of wisdom, of knowledge, of physics, of might, of joy—all power, all God, the power of the most and the least and in between. All power in heaven and earth is His. Aren't we glad that He understands the power of forgiveness, of letting go, and of gentleness, and that He shares His power with us?

Zechariah 4:6

Rest in contentment today as you remember who you are. To be a child of God means that you are more and more like him. His Spirit in you changes you, gives you more confidence that all things work together for your good. Take a few minutes to quietly listen, knowing His limitless power, knowing His unsurpassed ability to take the righteousness of "filthy rags" and transform it into a thing of great beauty, to take one who is unholy and make him pure, to take a "spirit of bondage" and make it one of freedom. Praise Him for who He is. Taking time to know who made you, loves you, and nurtures you gives you a sense of peace amid your busyness. The name of Jesus calms every storm when you know you belong to Him. The savory taste of the first fruits of your faith when you accepted the Lord as your Savior were only a foretaste of the harvest to come. The future securely holds its joys for you. What peace you find while sitting under the fruit trees of His grace receiving His gifts, His fruit!

Romans 8:14, 23, 28

What joy! Coming home means being who we are, being ourselves. Dancing a jig in the garage or in the yard may be in order. The rejoicing of the Israelites when they came home from Babylonian captivity must have been awesome to behold. They had seen the glory of the Lord, had experienced His mighty works in freeing them from captivity, and had understood that God knew their names as He does ours who have touched the hem of His garment.

In Christ we are at home, in confidence, peace, and love. We can dance on the walls of His kindness and goodness as they did, knowing that His joy is our strength, knowing we may be troubled for a while, but "joy comes in the morning." At these times we want to say, "God, bless God."

Nehemiah 8:10
Psalm 30:5

The ruling passion of Christ is His love for you. It is not the lukewarm feeling of an aloof friendship, but an intense, overmastering conviction that you were worth giving up everything He was so that you can live eternally. In return He asks that your driving force be an intense feeling and dedication to Him. The red envelope in your white mailbox with the yellow tulips around it contains the message from His heart. It is a love letter with words more authentic than any you have ever received. "Believe in me and I will give you the desires of your heart as you pray according to my perfect will. I will give you words of life," it says.

Is your faith genuine? The trials through which you go test and refine your faith. Faith is substance in God's kingdom. It is the stuff with which God's gold is bought—the wealth that can never be lost. He would have your genuine devotion, pure and true, so that you may wear the robe of white He purchased for you. His desire is to be the ruling passion of your life.

Revelation 3:4,18
John 11:6
Psalm 37:4

The rainbow's multicolored beauty paints an arc of promise in the sky. It is an arc that covers all of creation. It appears in the section directly opposite the sun, and God assures us that He will be there illuminating our world, revealing His truth in every situation. He who knows what is in the darkness disperses, refracts, and reflects its rays so that our breakthroughs may come. He who searches the heart knows the angle from which we need to see. Can any wrong thought hide itself in secret places when the Lord "fill(s) heaven and earth"? The infinite knowledge and understanding of almighty God enters the raindrops of our hearts, bends the light so that we see accurately, dividing and separating the blackness so that it becomes beautiful reds, oranges, yellows, greens, blues, indigos, and violets. His truth, His illumination, disperses our sorrows and turns them into joy. As David told Solomon, if you seek him, you will find Him who understands all "the imaginations of the thoughts." We need but ask Him to show us truth.

1 Chronicles 28:9
Jeremiah 23:24
Daniel 2:22
Romans 8:27

The zinnias blooming in the neighbor's garden always capture my attention as I pass. Their shades of orange, red, and yellow are varied and often unique. They make me thankful for the gift of sight. I can imagine the blind man that Jesus healed running and dancing up and down the streets; the one who had never seen before perhaps did not have a clue about what he was missing, but Jesus knew just as He knows what we are missing without the deeper vision. Perhaps it is that our vision must be muddied first, like the mixture of clay and Jesus's saliva that the man washed from his eyes. When asked who had healed him, the newly seeing man answered at first that He was a man, then he said He was a prophet, but because he insisted that Jesus was from God, he was "cast out." How amazing it must have been to this man that not only his seeing ability was given, but that Jesus returned to him to affirm that He is the Savior. How honored he must have felt to be able to say, "Lord, I believe!" and to actually see His physical presence and worship Him.

In the same way, our meeting the Lord follows the progression of seeing or knowing the physical, understanding the connection between "what is" and the creator, having the wisdom to accept the truth and being empowered to speak it as this man did. What a gift to be able to say, "Lord, You are the Christ, the Son of the Living God."

John 9

If Things are just so "iffy." Satan even presented Jesus with ifs: "If you are the son of God … If you will worship me." Jesus declared that He *is* the Son of God, that He *is* the Word that was before the world began and still *is*. He said that we are to worship the Lord God and Him only. *If*s are insecure, hesitating, not getting anything done. Definitiveness knows and accomplishes. Am I going to work at it or not? Am I going to graduate, or am I not? Until there is commitment, there is hesitation and usually failure. At the pool of Bethesda, a crippled man said basically, "*If* the angel will trouble the pool … and *if* someone will put me in, I will be healed." Jesus replied in essence, "Don't be iffy. You don't need the pool. You need me. Rise up and walk." Jesus is not the God of "iffy." He is God, God of everything. He is for you. Trust Him. Do as He says. Rise up and walk. Believe! You will be happier, have more peace, and be healed of your fear of accomplishing more and having more responsibility. Make the decision! Do it!

Luke 4:1–13
John 5:1–9

The Smallest Things

The deer nibbling the bushes in my yard, unaware of the eyes watching them, appear to be enjoying their breakfast. A feeling of security like theirs appeals to me. Psalm 18 finds David praising almighty God who "rode upon the cherubim," who "bowed the heavens," and trampled "darkness under His feet" to deliver David from his enemies. It was David's cry to God that initiated the release of His angels, that turned his world upside down so that righteousness prevailed.

Will God answer our prayers in such a way as He did David's, a man close to His heart? Yes! The most holy place of God, the place of intimate prayer guarded by angels, contains His mercy seat, the blood having been applied, the intercession for us made by the Son Himself. How awe-inspiring is the invitation to enter this place of great blessing and tremendous power to talk to Him about even the smallest things! The unleashing of His angels to protect my flower bushes is not too little for Him who knows whether seeing the deer or the flowers will bring me greater joy. Yes, we can be secure in His love for us. There is no need to worry. He has everything under control.

Psalm 18

The Good Shepherd

The good shepherd lies at the gate at night so that he may protect his sheep from the intrusion of wild beasts. The sheep need not worry about disturbances, nor do they need to fear being led to dangerous, rushing waters, for the good shepherd guides them to a place of rest and peace. The trickles that they hear are mere reminders of the shepherd's goodness. Though storms may rage around them, within the cave or pen is peace. In the days of burning sun, his hand covers them. His rod and staff guide them to the shady places where they are not alone, but enjoy his company and his provision. He is the Good Shepherd who gives His life for His sheep. Yes, Jesus, the Good Shepherd who protects and comforts His own, is more than enough. He is worthy of our trust.

Psalm 23, 49:2

The Shift in Focus

The sun shining through the morning mist calls us to the beauty of the day. Though the hay field's labor means being engulfed in sweltering heat, the martins glide and swerve around the tractor and the deer with its summer red coat pauses to share his beauty, and we are suddenly in tune with the magnificence of God. The shift in focus adds contentment and anticipation amid discomfort. What critters in their God clothes might show themselves? What life lies in the next turn of the wheel? It is the joy of the journey amid discomfort that we often find our Lord. Seeing Him is the reward for which we travail, the peace that money cannot buy. One glimpse reminds us of unseen things, things that last—the food the angel gave Elijah, which strengthened him forty days, the sealed work of Jesus Christ, which cannot be undone, love that never fails. The supply of the journey sustains us; the nibbles of angel food fuel our expectations, and we are replenished. How good our God is! May the smile in the eyes of a friend, a picture of summer beauty, the twitter of a bird, or other "small" thing sustain you today as you pause for a touch of His glory.

1 Kings 19:8
2 Corinthians 3:14
1 Corinthians 13:13
Luke 12:19,20

Come to the table. The food is plentiful, and the drink is nourishing. It is the food of peace and tranquility that Jesus eats with us now that the kingdom is in our hearts. As for the table rituals, our hands have been washed; the uncleanliness is gone. We have escaped death; the blood of the dead bird has been sprinkled as it was for the healed lepers in Leviticus, and like birds that have escaped death, we can fly through the fields of the Lord, pausing to rest under a grapevine or a fig tree. The feast that is ours is in stark contrast to the supper before Christ's death. Ours is not a somber meal where we know that crucifixion is yet to come, but a joyous feast in anticipation of the marriage supper of the Lamb. Let us praise Him, the giver of life.

Luke 22:18
Zechariah 3:10
Leviticus 14:7

He Has Come!

The hillside is covered with flowers, the lilies that neither toil nor spin. Jesus walks among them as they bloom by the river. They are His, nurtured by Him, the risen Lord. The restoration has come, and the glory that was His before the world began is His once again. The difference is that now you and I share in His glory. We are as a flower that does not have to worry but simply trust. Ours is the simple beauty swaying in the breeze. The storm may come outside, but within our hearts, Jesus walks among us, nurturing us and giving us peace as He does the flowers on the hillside. What is that smell? It is breakfast by the seashore. Who is that standing there? It is Jesus who has prepared it. Come; eat among the dew-embossed flowers that you so resemble. He has come. He will not leave.

John 17:5, 21:9
Luke 12:27

He Has Control

Sometimes it comes—the perfect day when the waves of the sea roll gently in and gently out like the soft waves of our lives when we are at peace. Sometimes on an unexpected stormy night, the wind rages as it did for the disciples on the Sea of Galilee. At these times we wonder where God is, why the storm is raging, and what we are to do. The great windstorm is always known by God. Though it may not be of His doing, He has control over it. Perhaps He is resting on the pillow in the stern waiting for you to seek His input. One thing we know for sure: He has control over the situation. All the elements of nature and humanity are under His control. Are we more afraid of the storm or of the power of the master of the storm who can direct its nature and path and who can direct ours? The fear comes when we think of turning over the control to God, but the result is peace. May you have peace today.

Mark 4:35–41

Renewal

Our Lord stands ready. In early spring sprouts begin to push through the dirt, reminding us of rebirth and renewal. The harshness of winter gives way to expectation. We are reminded that our Father's power is not necessarily as we think of it—not the strength of a horse as it storms the battlefield or of the winds and waves. His is also the power of spirit, of regeneration, of new life. His is the ability to bring such joy that the mountains and hills seem to "break forth into singing" and the trees "clap their hands." At such times, we know our Lord stands ready in the flower-laden field, reins in hand, not only to protect but to nurture His children, to preserve the new life He has given. How glad we are to be His, to be secure in His fields.

Isaiah 55:12
Revelation 19:11

The cool waters of Brasstown Creek flow lazily through the wooded bottoms on hot, summer days, giving definition to the words *calm* and *tranquil*. The creek's deceptive quiet allows us to forget that outside its shaded banks and beneath its surface, activity continues nonstop. Rocks block the water's path, and nature's critters within tend their business. In the distance cars and trucks hurry to their destination, and downstream beavers busy themselves gnawing bushes and trees for their dams.

Within ourselves, though, all is okay with the world. Our minds are thinking about good things—those that are true, noble, pure, lovely, virtuous, of good report, and praiseworthy. Such is the nature of peace. These deliberations that are of God renew our minds and strengthen our hearts. These meditations give no sway to the crying of "peace when there is no peace," for they recognize the enemies that attack our minds and bodies but know intimately the God who is in control of all things. Therein is our peace—that we have asked, that we trust the one who is worthy to be praised, that we are obeying, and that our focus remains on His goodness.

Philippians 4:7–9
Ezekiel 13:10

His Rest

The bottoms are beautiful this late summer morning, I thought as I straightened myself after clipping the weeds from the electric fence row and looked around. The queen of the meadow and the goldenrod stood tall and regal, bowing slightly with the breeze as if to show themselves courteous. The peace amid the busy flurry of bees and butterflies gave me pause. It seemed to come without effort. Peace, however, is a state of the heart that usually comes with pursuit; once present, it rests in naturalness. The sights and sounds of the present world seem busy and sometimes troublesome, but in Jesus we have peace.

What a difference He made to His own nation and the world. The Israelites were in constant dispute with other people because of their religion and their setting themselves apart, but Jesus came to bring the common bond of faith in Him. Outwardly, peace comes by being of one mind, pursuing healthy relationships, dealing with issues before they grow out of control, and showing courtesy, respect, and compassion. Inwardly, knowing that God is in control, that He cares, and that He is active in our lives gives us security in today and in tomorrow. Peace of heart calls us to immerse ourselves in His rest. It knows no worry. May you have peace today.

2 Corinthians 13:11–14
1 Peter 3:8–11
John 16:33

His Presence

Where is Jesus? He is not in a tomb for His remains to be found. The angel whose presence had been heralded by an earthquake and whose face was like lightning told Mary Magdalene and the other Mary that He had risen and was going before them into Galilee, their home. Jesus appeared to two of His disciples on the road to Emmaus. He also appeared to them in Jerusalem, where He showed the disciples His hands and side. They saw Him by the Sea of Galilee, where He cooked breakfast for them. They saw Him on the mountain in Galilee, where they worshiped Him and He told them to go into the world and teach. Here Jesus told them He would be with them always "even to the end of the world." At Bethany as He lifted His hands and blessed them, the disciples saw Him "parted from them and carried up into heaven." As Stephen was being stoned, he said, "Behold, I see the heavens opened, and the Son of Man standing at the right hand of God." There He speaks to the Father on our behalf. How then is it that He is with us today in our homes, on the road, in the city, by the sea as we are tossed to and fro, on the mountain, and in all the world? His Holy Spirit, which descended at Pentecost, dwells within the heart of every believer, permeates creation, and does the work of our Lord and our God. He is with us always—no matter what! His words will not pass away.

Matthew 24:35, 28:1–7
Luke 24:31, 24, 51
John 21:9
Romans 8:34

Turning to Jesus

The view is better from the top of the tower—the expanse broader, the destination clearer. Our Father's eyes see such things as the complete set of variables, the richer life, the meaning of struggles, and how victory is won. His spiritual vision understands how wars are fought. In whose hand would we rather place ours than in the hand of God who knows all, sees all, understands all. His victories are thorough, fought from the spiritual realm first and manifested in the physical world second. Trusting His greatness means remembering who He is, setting lesser avenues of help aside, turning to Him with a pure and complete heart. He is our refuge, our salvation, our health, and our strength. In Him, victory is sure to come regardless of our circumstance. Today we turn to the one who holds greater wisdom than all the collective understanding of humankind combined. More precious than rubies is one touch from His hand. Today we turn to Him.

Psalm 146:5
Proverbs 3:5

The Soft Voice

The happy sounds of birds chirping tell us that spring is coming once again. As cardinals and robins flit from limb to limb, we admire their quickness and their ability to land efficiently and keep their balance. Unlike these birds and unlike the meat-eating raven that Noah first sent out, the dove's soft, quiet coo reminds us of its purity, its diet of seeds and plants rather than dead meat. Its strong wings give it the self-control to light wherever it wishes. The Holy Spirit's descending like a dove on Jesus at His baptism speaks of a quiet, powerful confidence that comes from knowing. "You are to be like the dove," its appearing seemed to tell Jesus.

The Holy Spirit is not showy like an eagle or parakeet, but is the voice of strength. It is the inspiring, strong voice that James and John left their fishing boat and father to follow. It is the soft voice that healed the lame and raised the dead. It is the voice that told the woman at the well that she did not have to find another man to marry, but that she was already loved. It is the Spirit that Isaiah says will bring "justice to the nations ... He will not cry or lift up his voice." His power is not vicious and murderous but is used tenderly and meekly to heal and create enthusiasm. His is the quiet voice about which the Father said, "This is My beloved Son; listen to Him."

Isaiah 42:1–4
Mark 1:10, 20; 9:7

Finding Direction

Gliding through the water, the sailboat's beauty inspires romantic notions of smooth travel to sunny places and happy climes. Though sometimes the waves may rise and fall and the winds shift directions, the one whose rudder is controlled by the wise captain will reach its destination. He is the one whose steady anchor is in the wisdom of the ages, in the all-powerful, all-seeing, and everywhere-present God. Though the price of a gem-quality ruby is greater than the price of diamonds, the value of the person whose eye is on the Lord, the Master Captain, is far above it. In God's kingdom, which is within the Christian, wisdom supersedes emotion; the seeker finds healing in its "still, small voice" and gains focus. God Himself, who is wisdom, has spoken. After the sailor has heard Him speak, no longer is his sailboat going around in circles, for the Light on the horizon calls to him and he recognizes and values His instruction. May He who knows all control your direction, and may your sails feel the sweet breezes of His truth-filled breath today.

Proverbs 3:15, 31:10

The Master of Peace

The path strewn with debris testifies to the storm that was. From whose hand did the storm come? What was the cause, and what was the purpose? Such confused havoc having twisted through our lives, we welcome the sun's pleasant rays and a time to recover, to regroup, and to carry on. The still, small voice that comes after the storm and the wind is the one that makes sense. It is the voice of peace, of standing still in the presence of the great "I am" who simply is who He is in the midst of the fighting and wars and tornadoes. Though all the demons of hell struggle against Him, try to blow Him away, try to leave Him torn in pieces, He stands. The storm unleashed in your world cannot destroy the Master of Peace. He is there in the still, small voice speaking truth that frees you from worry. No longer do the boulders and splinters keep your spirit raw and bloody. Wounds heal, and joy reigns. These are the rewards of faith given by the One who works through love and would have you do so.

Galatians 5:6, 8

The Highway

When God breathes, creation comes to life: trees and grass turn green; flowers bud and bloom; and the sweet-smelling vines at first growing in the valley like a wave spread to the hills. Their growth reminds us of our own, the fresh days of childhood and youth, the maturing summer followed by fall and winter. Isaiah compares man to the grass. What of him or her lasts? A basic fact of life is the temporary quality of it and its riches. The Babylonians carried away the pride of King Hezekiah—gold, silver, armor, and precious ointment. All who were in his house, including his sons, were carried off to Babylon to be eunuchs in the king's palace. Hezekiah acknowledged that it was God's love for Hezekiah's soul that delivered him from the temporary nature of life. Jesus, who is the Word personified, said that the church is built upon the revealed word of God. The gates of hell—*death*—will not prevail against the lives of people of faith, those whom Jesus prayed that the Father would receive. Though the things of earth pass away, eternal spring reigns in the kingdom of God where all things are made new. His way is the unending "high way."

Revelation 21:1–8
2 Corinthians 5:17
Isaiah 40:3, 8
John 17:24

His Word Is Sure

Speaking "with" the Lord is no small matter. Those who touched the border of Mount Sinai when the Lord was giving the Ten Commandments to Moses would die even though they had cleansed themselves. However, today, because of the cleansing power of Jesus Christ when you were saved, you can hear His replies and rest on His word. In the give and take of conversation, God reveals truth to you that will not be compromised.

In the story of Joash, one of the Davidic kings, the clause, "God save the king," leaps from the page. He, a small child, was the only rightful heir to the throne who was left after Athaliah, in a bloody, power-hungry rampage, had killed all his siblings and would have killed him. The crisis, one of the highest points of tension in the history of Christianity, came when Jehoshabeath, the priest's wife, was able to hide him. Would God's promise to David that a Savior would be born through his family stand? Yes! This story illustrates the fact that no matter how bad the circumstances are, His word is sure, and He will honor His promises.

Luke 21:33
2 Chronicles 23:11

Scarlett O'Hara did not drip with righteousness when she went to see Rhett Butler, who was in prison after the Civil War. Her hands were rough from laboring in the gardens and fields, and she knew her beloved Tara, practically destroyed by Sherman's army, was on the auction block. In addition, she was tired of being hungry. At one point in the movie, *Gone with the Wind*, while pulling turnips from the ground, she raised her hands toward heaven and swore "as God is (was) my (her) witness" that neither she nor her family would ever go hungry again. Her mission involved luring Rhett into giving her money.

One might argue that Scarlett was strong and true in her motive to secure a place and food for family and servants. Regardless of her place along the goodness line, however, her righteousness was as "filthy rags" before God, as is ours. Paul, who suffered disasters, beatings, and tremendous hardship in his journeys to spread the gospel of Jesus realized that no goodness he ever did could stand sufficiently before God. God's great mercy clothes us more appropriately than dresses made from curtains that are meant to block the sun. In it we find the food and clothing that cannot be found at our "Taras." Mary found the answers at the feet of Jesus. That's where we should go—to sit at the feet of Jesus.

Zechariah 3:4
Philippians 3:3–10
Luke 10:39

Holding Your Hand

Did your heart not burn within you? When the sameness, the weariness, or the discouragement that you felt seemed never ending, while others seemed to prosper but you did not though you worked constantly, or when what you had worked for seemed to go up in smoke, was there not a faint stirring in your heart? The two men on the road to Emmaus after the Savior's death were discouraged. They had seen His works and had believed His miracles. Yet, He had died. Mary Magdalene, Joanna, Mary the mother of James, and the other women had told them of the empty tomb and of seeing the angels, but their words seemed as "idle tales." It had been too much—one discouragement after the other. Their worried reasoning and their trying to make sense of it all led through a dusty path in their minds not much different from the road upon which they were walking. When a stranger met them on the road, walked with them and talked with them, helping them to understand, it was not until He ate with them, when He blessed the bread and brake it that they recognized Him. Jesus had been there all along journey—He, the risen Savior who is alive and well.

Along your journey, has your heart not burned within? May He bless you today by opening your eyes to see that He has been there all along and is yet holding your hand.

Luke 24:11, 30–32

His Sanctuary

How does that song go? "Lord, it's hard to be humble when you're perfect in every way" (Mac Davis). Perfection means faith and trust in Him who embodies no evil. It means peace, lying down to sleep at night knowing the Lord holds us in His safe hands. Regardless of the enemies that may surround us, we find our safety in Him who is our righteousness and who prevails on our behalf against deceit and vengeance. Our own perfection is "as filthy rags" regardless of how close to being flawless we may seem to be. It is His whose name is excellent in all the earth, His name that personifies goodness in all the works of His hands. At the mention of His name, *"Every* knee shall bow ... and *every* tongue will confess ..." that He is the Lord of all the earth, in control of everything. Deceit and wickedness are revealed at the mention of His name, and His children are delivered. God's chosen, "peculiar" people need not toss and turn in their beds in worry because He hears when they call. His sanctuary is ever open to those who do so. It is the place where God's way is found, the place of unity and peace.

Deuteronomy 14:2
Philippians 2:10
1 Peter 2:9

Logic

What philosophies find logic in senseless killings of numerous people? What religions account for the evil in man or his weaknesses? What theories hold the eternal truths of life? Through the ages humankind has rationalized. Regardless of whether their dogmas hold some correct thinking, the teaching of Christianity that Jesus gave Himself as a substitute for my sins stirs my soul and assures me of its truth. That He did so defies logic, all philosophy, and the sophisticated thinking of man. Its reality cuts through layers of learning, speculation, and emotion where the truths of Jesus touch the inner core of our being. Life is about who He is, about His love for us, and about who we are in Him. It is about the freedoms inherent in a life lived according to His teachings. It is about freedom from hate. Where is the sunshine in hate and in its related attitudes of resentment, insecurity, death? Along with Charles Spurgeon and Beth Moore, I say that there is none. "Just give me Jesus."

1 Corinthians 1:19

Let All that I Have

David's harp that praised the Lord has ceased its vibrations, and Solomon's 120 trumpeters sound their horns no more, yet praise still opens the doors through which the King of glory comes. The sounds of musical instruments alone are insufficient, but the voice of the heart that says, "He indeed is good for His lovingkindness is everlasting" is the one that invites the Holy Spirit to stir within the heart and to move in the world.

The door of heaven that opened to receive the Savior had seen the ultimate praise of Jesus, who had praised God with the sacrifice of His life. The same door opens to hear the praise of the child who believes. Praise is the message of the humble who say that God is greater, kinder, more loving, more gracious, more powerful, and worthier than anyone else in heaven and on earth. Unified hearts grown bigger with the love of God and hands lifted in joyous praise see the entrance of the King, who has Himself opened the doors. What joy to be in that chorus that uplifts their voices to say, "Worthy is the Lamb that was slain to receive power and riches and wisdom and might and honor and glory and blessing." May your heart be filled with the joy of praise today.

2 Chronicles 5:11–13
Psalm 24:7
Revelation 5:13

Has God forgotten you? No! As He did not forget His chosen people who had been carried off into Babylon, He does not forget His own today. The day of Zechariah's prophecy came when the Israelites shone like jewels in a crown and were lifted like a banner over the land waving the message of victory. After seventy years in captivity, they had returned to Jerusalem, the Holy City, to rebuild the temple where God had promised to meet them. Our Savior has come and given His children a place of honor, ever lifting their banner before the Father.

No longer are God's people in a place like a "waterless pit," where we cannot hear God's voice, but we are in the presence of our Lord, who is always working and who is always speaking encouragement to His own. The still, small voice you hear holds words of hope. Following its leading will carry you to victory. He who called you by your name is speaking. Do you hear His voice? Is He speaking through others? Are circumstances showing you a way of hope? What scripture passages are drawing you into the Living Word? He who is speaking to you has not forgotten.

Zechariah 9:12, 16

Jesus Sings

Jesus sings! The abandoned house once occupied by the birds and wild animals is now filled with song. It is the time of restoration for the children of the king. Though you may have experienced troubles along with the other people of the earth, the voice of our Savior resounds through the hearts and homes of you, the remnant, who believe. The songs that echo in your hearts, minds, and souls are not the cries of birds and beasts, but the creative and restorative words of Jesus, who sings with joy over your faith.

Imagine His sweet healing voice permeating every atom of your being. As you rejoice at the thought of being eternally saved from the enemy and at the thought of being cherished by the King, He sings words of blessing and honor over you as He did Abraham and Sarah. You who have not cut yourself off from fellowship with God have found the source of happiness. The spiritual land of promise is yours. Singing with Jesus in mutual love, you hear the direction of Him whose melodious voice lifts because of you.

Zephaniah 2:14, 3:17
Genesis 12:1–3

God's Loyal Love

Regardless of the condition you are in, God's loyal love will not fail you as you abide in Him. When the Israelites wandered in the wilderness not knowing what to do, God gave them direction. When the apostles were in prison, "an angel of the Lord opened the prison doors and brought them out." When the five thousand were physically hungry by the shores of Galilee, He fed them. When He saw that they were also like sheep without a shepherd, He fed their hungry souls. When Mary Magdalene was filled with seven demons, He delivered her. When the disciples were caught in a storm on the sea, Jesus came walking on the water. When there was no more wine at the wedding in Cana, Jesus turned the water into wine. When the seventy that Jesus sent out felt powerless, Jesus performed miracles through them, and they returned with joy. When the woman with the issue of blood had spent all her money on physicians, Jesus healed her. When Elijah felt alone, believing he was the only one left who honored God, God revealed to him that there were seven thousand more. The blessing these people received was not the deliverance itself, but the knowledge of the Deliverer. Abiding in Jesus means that you hear His teaching and allow Him to bless you according to His riches in glory.

Psalm 107
Joshua 6:6
1 Kings 19:10
Acts 5:19
John 6:16–21
Luke 1:41–44, 8:2

Compassion

As the sun peeps through Crow Gap into Young Harris Valley, life is already buzzing. A business or two has opened its doors, the college has begun its lessons, and smoke rises from a chimney in the cove to the northwest. Cars speeding in the distance breaking the calm seem adverse to the natural mountain life as the streams roll peacefully and the deer retreat from picking grass in the fields to the woods. As one answers the call to duty focused on the day ahead, God's compassion is no less than in quiet times when the soul reflects upon it. Leviticus describes God's promise that He will appear in a cloud of mercy after a scapegoat has symbolically carried their sins into the wilderness. How much more will his compassion encircle those who are covered by the blood of His own Son, who carried man's sins to the cross? Outwardly engrossed in the necessity of the day's clamor, within we can be at peace knowing that our merciful God constantly watches over us even though we cannot focus on Him. May the peace in your heart give you clarity of mind as you go about your work today.

Leviticus 16:3, 10

The Outfit You Are Wearing

How lovely is the outfit you are wearing, dear Christian, for it radiates the love of God. As a child of the Most High, your cloak is not the knee-length, short-sleeved, and plain apparel of the poor, but the long-sleeved, ankle-length, and colorful one worn by royalty. Its multiple colors shine with His righteousness, His covering, and His victory. Though you may use this valuable attire as the Hebrews did—to protect from the weather, to sit upon, as a bag to carry belongings, or as a blanket to cover yourself at night—it is Jesus who protects you from the storms of life, His word that you stand upon, He who holds your treasures, and He who covers you with light in dark places. Ripping your robe into two pieces as a show of your grief is unnecessary, for the Lord Himself carries your grief. The soldiers who cast lots for Jesus's garment did so because it was woven into one piece with no seams. His covering is not piecemeal but complete. No one can take away the robe of righteousness that God has given you; no one can take away your hope or your covering. In the Savior, you are secure and beautiful.

Genesis 37:3
Exodus 22:26
Isaiah 61:10
John 19:23

Christ in You

The great mystery of God has drawn the attention of man since the dawn of time. Genesis tells us that He created man in His image and made us beings who have the ability and freedom to choose Him or evil. He is one of the choices at the end of "either/or." In other Old Testament books, we find that He is our provider, our strength, our victory, our shepherd, our peace, our righteousness. John tells us that God desires to show His glory through us as He did the blind man who had not sinned, nor had his father, but he was born blind "so that the works of God might be displayed in him." In Christ, we saw the embodiment of love. At Pentecost, we find that He became the rushing mighty wind within us, enabling us to do things that are humanly impossible. Our God would have us know Him, experience Him, and be a conduit of His revelation of Himself. He is God who pours out His Spirit so that we see "wonders in heaven above, and signs in the earth beneath" and so that His sons and daughters proclaim His revealed word. He is the God who calls us to see Him as He keeps His focus on every detail of our lives. He is the God who loves and cares for you.

Zechariah 2:8
Acts 2:2, 4, 17, 19
John 9:1–3
Colossians 1:27–28

Butterflies

That viburnum bush outside my door is not too particular about where it grows, a fact my not-too-green thumb appreciates. Yellow swallowtail, little blue azure, and brownish elfin butterflies flit from pinkish flower to whitish flower to pinkish flower, covering the bush with their busyness, their varied stripes, dots, zigzags, and shades of color. They, no doubt, like the sweet-smelling nectar unleashed by its blooms. That one is not a monarch evidently makes no difference to this bush, for its fragrance summons all. The botanist says it grows in all kinds of places: wet or dry, sun or shade, natural or formal, native or exotic. It blooms at different times, and in the fall its leaves are varying shades of gold and red. Leaves may be rounded, lance-shaped or toothed, smooth, velvety or rough. Jesus is like that bush. He blooms in all kinds of places, calling His children with all their differences to a beautiful, nourishing, varied life. It's okay if I'm not a monarch.

Acts 10:9–15

Hope

More varied than the spotted patterns of the Appaloosa, one of America's favorite horses, are the mercies of our God. As the new day dawns, so does the freshness of His grace. The hope that broadens our view and takes us out of our natural musings empowers us to wait upon the Lord. Waiting upon His timing with confident expectation is the seed of success and joy, for He is their keeper. What pattern will spring's foal have? The colt newly born soon bounces across the field, parading his unique coat. Whether snowcap, snowflake, leopard, mottled, or frost, the Creator has brought to fruition a beautiful creature that has been used for man's benefit and joy for centuries. The gifts of today are there for the noticing, for the enjoying, for the blessing, and for the showing of God's faithfulness. Where is the success of today and the hope for tomorrow? Who has the words of life but Jesus? To whom may we turn but Him? Waiting upon the Lord and noticing His mercy means that the new day will not be exactly as you planned; it will be richer.

John 6:68
Lamentations 3:22–23

The People of God

In John Steinbeck's book *The Grapes of Wrath*, the Joad family loses their farm and travels through California, trying to live as migrant farm workers. After much heartache and struggle, Ma Joad finds her strength and expresses it: "We're the people that live. They can't wipe us out; they can't lick us. We'll go on forever, Pa, 'cause we're the people." She refers to not only the heart's strength of the people, but the numbers also. It is in Christ that we will live forever. It is in Christ that "they" can't "lick" us. We are the people of God, individually valued to the extent that the Lord of heaven calls us to constant communion with Him. Just as God saw every person from Oklahoma and Arkansas as they faced the challenge to live, God sees our daily hills and mountains, and the depth and breadth of our need for Him. You are a unique being in God's array of journeying children. He will not fail you. His is the hand that holds you above the battles of the day in peace and assures you that in His-sweet smelling savor is life and life more abundantly.

John 4:31–38, 10:10
Psalm 21:6, 131:2

Wait

God, who watches over you, does not sleep soundly or take naps. More attentive and diligent than the watchmen placed in the towers built into the walls of ancient cities and castles or the combined surveillance of all the CIAs of the world, He sees all. Towers built to guard materials, families, and friendships, like the Tower of Babel, pale, crumble, and fall in comparison to the eyes and armor of God. Having called upon Him who is "the God of [your] rock … [your] shield … the power of [your] salvation, [your] high tower, [your] refuge, [your] savior who saves [you] from violence," wait. Like Habakkuk, having called upon the Lord, watch and listen in eager anticipation, for His answer will come. Do you see it? How will He respond to your reasoning about your concerns? How are you to interpret and understand His answer? Be patient, knowing the answer will come. He who knows all will reveal it to you.

Psalm 121:4
Habakkuk 2:1
2 Samuel 22:3, 51

Through Layers of Rubble

The tears of God's children are not only seen but remembered by God, who shall "wipe away all tears from their eyes." David prays that God would put his tears into a bottle, that He would notice them and remember them. Whatever the reason for them—stress, pleasure, anger, sadness, suffering, repentance—God hears the cries of His people. We can envision God hearing Jonah, who cried from "the belly of Sheol," through layers of earth—whale skin, thousands of feet of water, mountains of dirt and rock, miles of sky. Wherever we are beneath layers of trouble, God hears us. The turning comes in our distress when we reach the point of praising God in the midst of our trials. When our eyes turn back in humility and repentance, seeking His face, God can restore us to the correct path, to the attitude of trust that "if I perish, I perish." It is okay because we are in His hands, which are mightier, more knowing, and more caring than ours.

Revelation 21:4
Isaiah 25:8
Psalm 56:8
Jonah 2:2

The Giver

As the gift of Jesus Christ has passed through the corridors of time, so does His eternal peace, joy, and love. What a storehouse our God shares with us in that He gives us the giver and not just the gift. In the movie *Gone with the Wind*, Mr. O'Hara says, "'Tis the land, Katie Scarlett. It's the only thing that lasts." However, John tell us that heaven and earth shall pass away, but His Word shall not pass away. He is the Word, the thing that lasts. In Him we continue also. Christmas is such a joyous time because we know we have been given eternity. Having been given extraordinary treasure, we can only stand in amazement as "His train fills the temple," that is the Spirit within us. The quality is such that the more we give away, the more we have to give. We who have nothing to give but Jesus have everything. How blessed we are in this and every season!

Matthew 24:35
John 1:1
Isaiah 6:1

In His Garden

The gardens of the Lord are beautiful beyond measure. The varieties of herbs, flowers, fruits, and vegetables, with their aromas, colors, and shapes, are countless. In His garden is the answer for your every need. Isaiah says that if your genuine love comes through in your kindness and service to those around you, you will be "like a watered garden, and like a spring of water, whose waters fail not." His waters are life giving, for they spring up in your very essence, the center of your being. He "satisfies the longing soul, and fills the hungry soul with goodness" from the wealth of His gardens. Such beauty of being comes from being in His healing presence. Because you are born of Spirit, your life's joys and hopes originate in God. To Him, the repairer of the breach, we turn for healing and restoration.

Isaiah 58:11
Psalm 107:9

The Lion

The fluffy gray cat that peers at me from the windowsill as the wind blows its fur, no doubt, thinks he's mighty fierce. Those claws hold the promise of revenge if anyone tries to steal his food. Though he is not aware of it, the roaring lion within him has been reduced to a barely perceptible meow. A lion is a powerful beast. One imagines him as he walks almost leisurely, but confidently around his prey, his sharp teeth covered by furry skin. He is the brave hunter who can leap several yards at a single bound, who lurks in secret places, who does not turn away when facing danger, and who never leaves the trail as he hunts his prey. Nothing causes his whelps to be afraid, for he "tears in pieces" sufficient food for them and "strangle(s) for his lionesses."

In the same way, Jesus, the great Lion of Judah, feeds and protects His children and His bride, the church. Though a multitude of evil come against Him, He will not hide for "He will not be afraid of their voice." As a mighty lion protects his prey, our Lord protects the person who has given his life to Him. The enemy cannot leap far enough, cannot hide himself enough, cannot be brave enough, and cannot have enough stamina to outlast the Lion of Judah. Though He may appear to be casually walking oblivious to all our issues, no matter the dilemma, let us not be deceived. He will prevail.

Nahum 2:11–12
Isaiah 30:4

The consistent beauty of your inner spirit pleases God. Like a walnut with its rough, hard shell, the fruit within is the treasure. Jesus describes Himself as a "pearl of great price" that one is willing to give everything he has so he may own it. Jesus knew human nature to the extent that He did not entrust Himself to anyone. When people Jesus had healed talked too much, He silenced them. When followers tried to make Him king, His kind, consistent words revealed a greater kind of king. Rather than human nature, which is man's fallible possession, true richness is faith and love within the heart. Its genuineness does not "do alms before men" or for praise, though others see its outward manifestation. Like the virtuous woman of Proverbs 31 whose outward beauty is never mentioned, your strength is grounded in the Lord Himself. Your character shows in your wisdom, skills, and compassion—all of which come from the Pearl of Great Price within you. The Proverbs woman was not only honorable in her home but in the business world. So are you who carry the love of God with you. Be blessed.

John 2:24
Matthew 6:1
Proverbs 31
1 Peter 3:2

Prosperity

Our cat seems to be flourishing on the front porch, which she has chosen to be her home. It became her house when our dog, an Australian shepherd, decided it was his job to keep her "herded." How amusing to see her watch for him and then, when he isn't there, sneak off the steps and into the woods. Yesterday, after a couple of years of being around him, she lay curled on his long-haired breast. Her definition of prosperity, I believe, is plenty of food and peace with the dog. For humans it is, of course, more complicated. Flourishing does not mean loads of money, although some is required to live. It means peace and contentment, which come from placing our trust in the Lord. As long as Uzziah sought the Lord "in the days of Zechariah, who had understanding of the visions of God," he prospered. Hezekiah sought God in every work he did and "did it with all his heart," and he prospered. Without God, our hearts faint. Looking to the past and the situations through which He has brought us assures us that all is well and He has sent the Shepherd, the comforter of our souls, to keep us safe and at ease.

2 Chronicles 26:5, 31:21

The brilliant oranges, yellows, and reds of fall paint an amazing world. Pausing to bask in its abundance leaves the jolting thought that the colors were there all along, concealed by chlorophyll's greenery. How reassuring to realize that our Comforter and Keeper has been there all along enriching our lives. Zacharias is one who came to such a realization. Having not had the desired child that was considered such a blessing, the one that would take care of him in old age, Zacharias could not believe that he would have a son as the angel, Gabriel, said he would. Perhaps he had given up faith that God would bless him. How exhilarating it must have been for him to realize that God had been there all along, awaiting the appropriate time to birth John the Baptist, the "prophet of the Highest ... to give knowledge of salvation." Zacharias's inability to hear or speak until the child was born is a tremendous lesson in humility, a lesson in believing that God can and that He will though He has not yet and though now it seems impossible. Humility yields to belief that God has it totally under control, that He cares most about your relationship with Him, and that He will come through for you. He has been there all along.

Luke 1:18–25

Boxes

The boxes we build for God cannot contain Him. Solomon knew that fact when he built the temple and when, as the king, he knelt before all the people of Israel to worship and to pray. God's thoughts are not our thoughts. His creativity answers our needs and concerns in ways we never dreamed. We may be looking for doctors to perform healing techniques, and the healing may come in our hearts, or miraculously or ... We may be asking for material things, and He gives us something much greater than physical wealth.

The boxes we build for God limit His work in our lives because they often, in reality, illustrate a lack of faith. Our job is to know and truly believe that He will fulfill our needs. The what's and how's are His business. He said, "How often would I have gathered (you) ... under my wings ... and you would not" for lack of simple trust and belief. As the priests took, the ark of the covenant (a box) into the Holy of Holies, symbolically the innermost court or presence of God, they laid the promise of His covenant before Him. They were in effect saying, "As you promised us, we promise You. We meet You here at the promise." The implication is always that we will worship and believe to the best of our abilities, for only He can truly never fail. As we pray the promise, "God, You said You would never leave us or forsake us," we can rest assured that He never will and the "resting assured" is His only requirement for His fulfilling His promise. Keeping Him in a box illustrates lack of faith.

2 Chronicles 5:7, 6:13
Matthew 23:37
Hebrews 13:5

The Light

He is the sun that glitters as it reflects from the wet surface. How encouraging that God's light is so great that we cannot look directly, but see it only by reflection. Genesis tells us that once clothed in darkness, the abyss, the nothingness experienced God's light as He looked upon it. It is the darkness that pre-exists rather than the light as evening comes before the morning. Into such a void, Jesus came shining light into the darkness, making clear that His is the light of love. It is the hurt, pain, and anxiety we experience before the breakthrough comes, before His joy splits the veil.

We were not born for darkness. The light in an individual is His focus, the rays that He wants to broaden. He sees His goodness within, and when we see more of His in return, ours grows. Our healing grows into health that only He can provide and our happiness into joy. In the end, there is no end of the light, for God Himself is the light of the eternal city. His presence retains the fruit for which He has labored, its freshness never waning, and its vibrancy eternal. Be encouraged today.

Genesis 1:5
John 8:12
Revelation 21:23

Revision

Standing on the Mount of Olives looking across the Kidron Valley to Jerusalem, I have the feeling that time is standing still. It is a world of tans and grays. The ancient tombs that cover the descent into the valley are stark reminders of lives passed—of Absalom, Zechariah, and Habakkuk. How aware of death the apostles must have been as they looked across the half-mile stretch from Bethany to Jerusalem and as they listened to Jesus say that He was leaving and that it was not for them to know when He would return. His message to them was that they should not focus on death, but on life—not on the dead, but on the living. They would be given power when the Holy Spirit came to testify to the living of what they had seen. What they had seen was the awesome glory of the risen Savior, had seen all kinds of miracles, and heard amazing teaching regarding the spiritual and physical, and their relation to each other. Jesus said, "I will not leave you comfortless," and "I will come again." How surprised they must have been at the joy they felt at His ascension, for He was leaving. The anticipation of seeing Him again, of experiencing the fullness of abundant life without tombs, depression, and negativity, took away all fear. Life in Christ means keeping your focus on life.

Acts 1:4–11

Second Chances

Our God gives second chances. He who searches for you searches your heart. The One who leaves the ninety-nine who are safe to find the lost sheep also seeks to keep you close and in fellowship with Him. Conversely, humbly holding God close allows you to hear His voice and draws you to obey the voice that keeps you in love. Such love was given to Naaman, a Syrian, who had leprosy. After seeking to be healed by Elisha, about whom his servant had told him, Naaman found it difficult to obey Elisha's instructions to dip in the Jordan River seven times. His preconceived idea of how the healing would occur and the dirty Jordan held him back, but at his servant's encouragement, he did as he had been told. His healing drew him to a humble, repentant relationship with God and created a heart of obedience. Though he did not initially obey, God gave him a second chance and he was healed. More importantly, he came to know a loving and forgiving God.

Psalm 51:17, 34:18
2 Kings 5:1–19

Songs of Joy

Today is the day of rejoicing for those who have been invited to the wedding feast and are wearing the wedding garments. These are the clothing of the believer whose faith has prepared him to partake in the joys of the Lord. No longer is it the time of singing songs of lament. The battle is won; the path is set. As Deborah sang in her victory song after defeating Jabin, "You who travel on the road"—sing, sing the praises *of* the Lord, declaring to the world his graciousness.

The world without Jesus is a world without the music of a deep joy, but singing *to* the Lord is the communication of worship that lifts the singer higher into His presence. The world does not understand such music, for the prepared sing even in times of trouble, knowing the joy of the Lord is his hope and strength. It is the sound that wipes away the spirit of defeat. The gift of such music flows from the love of Christ who gave "Himself for us, an offering and a sacrifice to God." His love is not to be worked for, but believed in. It is the gift of unmerited favor, the gift of praise, the gift of music.

Ephesians 5:1
Matthew 22:1–14
Judges 5:10

As winter deepens into colder colds and the gray mountains grow starker, we find ourselves longing for the verdant spring mountains topped with grasses, trees, and wildflowers. They are miracles of growth that never cease to amaze. How could such beauty grow on rocks? Being rooted in the rock as they sometimes are means a crevice is created through which flow the materials of growth. The nutrients feeding such growth are provided by the path setter Himself, He who directs the upward path. Like grapevines that produce the finest wines, the Christian life flourishes in such a place founded upon the rock for the nutrients for its growth flow from the actual throne room of God. A person so rooted has the capacity for compassion for His salvation is secure. His being rests in the bowels of God from where mercy flows. Thus, he answers the demand Jesus made: "I will have mercy not sacrifice." What He has given is to be multiplied through the giving it away like the ever-replenished waters drawn into the clouds to be released to give life again. The responsibility of salvation is mercy—kindness above what may be expected or demanded by fairness. It is mercy that gives life to the giver and receiver.

Matthew 12:9

What a Savior!

Jesus was not good looking, yet people are drawn to Him. He was a man of sorrows, yet He brings joy. The hate of the world was upon Him, yet He loves without restraint. He grieved because of unbelief, yet He carries our grief. He had brothers and sisters, yet He calls you and me His family. He lived in poverty, yet feeds millions. He was oppressed but delivers us from oppression. He died a criminal's death, yet He is our righteousness. He was the victim of violence, yet He brings peace. He went like a lamb to the slaughter, yet He is captain of the angelic hosts of heaven. He succumbed to death on the cross, yet gives eternal life. He yielded to defeat, yet reigns in victory. He carried the wounds of vicious lashes, yet He is our healer. Paradoxically, He bore the burdens of the world so that the burdens would be no more. He was born in a lowly manger, but will return the Lord of Lords and King of kings. He holds our today and our tomorrows. Because of Him we have the fruit of the Spirit—love, joy, peace, forbearance, kindness, goodness, faithfulness. What a Savior!

Isaiah 53:2–10
Revelation 19:16

God's Glory

Glory refers to an abundance or magnificence not fully seen but suggested. Snatches of it are sometimes seen in the achievements of people and in the beauty of nature. Philip expressed man's deepest desire which is to see God's glory when he said to Jesus, "Show us the Father." Jesus explained that He is the Father: "He who has seen me has seen the father." His presence was different in that He had emptied Himself of the glory of the Father to become a man, though He had not given up the deity or reality of who He is. Thus, Jesus prayed that God would restore to Him the glory He had with the Father before the world was.

To show us His glory is to show us His presence as He did in the cloud as the Israelites traveled through the desert, in the ark of the covenant, and in Solomon's temple. Every miracle Jesus performed as He walked the earth and every miracle He does now is a revelation of His awesomeness. We know of His glory when we empty ourselves of humanity and invite the Holy Spirit to fill our hearts, minds, and souls. Having the mind of Christ, we live in love, humility, and unity. What honor He has shown us that we can glimpse His glory, one beyond compare, and have the Christ, the hope of glory, living in us.

Philippians 2:5–7
John 14:8, 17:5

By Reflection

Ezekiel uses the word *rainbow* in his description of the glory of God. Inherent in this word is the multiplicity of God's virtues, riches, and abilities, which are beyond counting. When David felt alone and friendless because his friends had followed his rebellious son, Absalom, God was his "shield," his protector. When David had nothing, God was his treasure. When no one was there to encourage him, God was his friend and sustainer. From nothingness, the great Creator God brings forth the riches of his storehouse. When Moses was discouraged and in despair, he said, "Lord, please show me Your glory." In the building of the temple at Jerusalem, God brought together talents from the gentiles and riches from the kings and queens of the earth who came "proclaim(ing) the praises of the Lord." Isaiah told Israel, "Arise, shine, for your light has come and the glory of the Lord is risen upon you." The diverse wealth of the King of the Ages is showered upon the kingdom of God within each of us. The time has come to ask Him to show His glory, for rejoicing in His presence, for children of the kingdom to show by reflection the glory of its Creator to a world gone awry.

Isaiah 60:1, 6
Ezekiel 1:28
Exodus 33:18
Psalm 3:1–5

Rising above Fear

Fears are weights that make the journey tedious and oppressive. Jesus said, "Come to me, all you that labor and are heavy laden and I will give you rest." David gives witness to the fact that His promise is true. David sought the Lord, and the Lord delivered him from all his fears, fears that were well grounded since Abimelech was seeking to destroy Israel.

As that experience is true of David, it is true of all those who seek the Lord. The angels camp or remain around those who look to God. David tells us that the eyes of the Lord are upon the righteous, those who believe in Jesus who is our righteousness. His ears are open and listening for their cry. Though fears are just emotions, uncontrolled. They guide and determine our steps. God calls us to rise above the fears that hold us down. Because he sought God, David was able to glimpse the cross for he prophesied that not one of Jesus's bones would be broken. They who look to Him will be able to "see the king in his beauty." He is the Prince of Peace. When you talk to him about it, you will see peace.

Psalm 34:4, 7, 15
Isaiah 33:17
Matthew 11:28

Expectation

Who is with us in the storms of life makes all the difference. The face of a trusted friend decreases the stature of the giant looming before us. A true friend's identity sometimes eludes us, however. As it was for the disciples traveling from Bethsaida to Capernaum when a storm arose, fear comes when we do not recognize the true giant. When Jesus came walking on the water, they were afraid. Their thinking He was a ghost brought Him down to terms they could vaguely understand, though it produced great fear. Had they expected Him, His appearance would not have caused such upset, but then, why would they expect Him? Who can walk on water? When they saw who He was, they "willingly received Him into the ship."

Underestimating the Master of the Storm leads to non-acceptance of His miracles and limitation of His work in our lives. Yet, how can our limited knowledge comprehend God who "hath measured the waters in the hollow of His hand"? It is He who "sit(s) upon the circle of the earth," who in all His power, knowing, and presence loves us, cares about us, holds us in the palm of His hand. His appearance in the middle of our storms is a tremendously small thing to Him. Why is our expecting it so difficult?

Isaiah 40:12, 22
John 6:16–21
Job 9:8

Welcoming Jesus

The straight-backed wooden chair on the porch or the cushioned one in the living room appeals to the tired, home from work or travel. Its seat has "welcome" written all over it. "You, who have done your service for the day," it says, "take your rest." It is not the seat of a king, but it is the seat the King has prepared for you, His servant. The word *servant* often means "one who is in training." High schools and vocational schools often call this situation "work-based learning." Thus, we are in training for heaven and for the Most High God, for the position to which He has called us. Occupying the chair as His servant holds prestige and honor. Jesus said that He no longer calls us "servants" when we do as He asks, but He calls us "friends," friends for whom He was willing to give everything.

The Shunamite woman recognized Elisha as a servant of God; thus, she fixed a small upper room—with a bed, table, lampstand, and *chair*—for him to use when he passed her house. Recognizing people in our lives for who they truly are makes all the difference in how they're treated. Those who have accepted God's grace are all His servants. Jesus is sometimes referred to as the "suffering servant." His "chair" in our hearts is a special place, one where He delights in talking to us as He rests. It's a good time to make sure the welcome sign is dusted and the doors of our hearts are opened.

2 Kings 4:10
John 15:15

Blundering

Did you ever make a foolish mistake that embarrassed you or caused problems? Biblical words for that experience are *blundering* and *stumbling*. Interestingly the English version of *blundering* is not in the Bible, but Abishag's name meant "blundering." She was the woman who lay with King David as he was dying, to keep him warm. Discretion is a close opposite of "blundering." Ironically Abishag's "job" probably required that she be wise, keep confidences, and be often silent in her behavior and service—be discreet. How difficult those things can be!

Proverbs says that we should keep "sound wisdom and discretion; so they will be life to your soul and grace to your neck ... and your foot will not stumble." Like a long-necked dinosaur, I could use a little grace. Those feet get awkward carrying around such "foolishness." Abishag, the beautiful woman chosen to serve the king, was given the grace to answer her calling. Though she may have been a blunderer, God gave her what she needed. His love is always sufficient.

1 Kings 1:3, 15, 2:17, 21–22
Proverbs 3:21–23

Being unique, as you are, means no one exactly like you exists on the face of the earth, a fact that can be both comforting and scary. When God called you by your name before you were in the womb, He must have thought about how you would respond to His call to the task He had planned for you. I can imagine Jonah, for example, saying, "No! No! No, God! I will not go to Nineveh. They are our enemies. You know what they will do to me." I can imagine him in the belly of the whale trying to wipe half-digested fish out of his face and trying to regain a sense of orientation and power. At some point, perhaps while the whale was swimming through the Strait of Gibraltar, he must have said something like, "Okay, God. You are sovereign God. My life is not my own. I will tell them you are God and that they must repent. Just don't let me be digested in this messy place." Most likely, it was at this point of acknowledging that his life did not belong to him, but to God, that Jonah's fate changed.

God's call for you, like Jonah's, has your individuality at the forefront, yet, as the Bible heroes illustrate, all great accomplishment acknowledges the all-powerful God and the frailty of man. How difficult it is to let go of the power you think you have and do as He leads! On the other hand, how comforting it is to know that He will take care of you as you "walk" in the truth that His every act toward His children has love at its core.

2 John 6
Jonah 1:17, 2:7

Enthusiasm

Remember those carefree days of childhood when we skipped through the yard with such physical agility? In more recent times, the art of skipping may have left us though the pattern of life may not have. Sometimes we go sailing through the air; sometimes we hit the ground on one foot or the other. The expanse of sailing depends upon the strength and energy that goes into the shove from the ground. Though the leg muscles be strong, the enthusiasm for the jump determines its span. Fraught with the repetitiveness of our everyday actions or "the daily grind," zeal for the task often dulls.

John talks about the Laodicean church, whose members were wealthy as a result of their self-confident pursuits, which they regarded with pride. Focus on one's self as the source, however, limits possibilities. These people had become as tepid as the water that flowed into the city from the hot springs some distance away. They were bland, forgetting that true gold, real spiritual treasures, can only be bought from Jesus. From him we get medicine to heal our eyes so that we may see things of true and lasting value. Truths that open the world of possibility lengthen the time in the air, the stretch of the skip, because we know that with God all things are possible. Happy sailing today!

John 15:5, 8
Matthew 19:26
Revelation 3:15

The Letter God Wrote

The letter God wrote on your heart changed you for all time. Your hands say that you are older now, but the light in your eyes sparkle with new birth. The challenges that you have faced would have marred a dinosaur, yet your skin is baby's-butt smooth. Puzzling experiences that you have had might have perplexed Einstein, but understanding simply flows through your mind. You have been ill-treated, but your face shines with the light of friendship. You have been put down, but your walk parades victory. Your lips need but say one word to express the transformation— *Jesus*. It is He who energizes your steps, He who walks with you through life's valleys, giving you resilient skin, He who lets you "just know" things, He who assures you that you are loved and valuable, He who fills you with the Spirit of life, and He who gives you words to speak of Him. Yes, you are changed. The life in you is beautiful.

2 Corinthians 4:7–12

Manna

The smell of freshly baked bread flowing from Mama's kitchen made home feel like an even friendlier and more welcoming place. It seemed to say, "We have tasty food and all is well." However, as the physical manna was not enough to satisfy the hunger of the Israelites in the desert, neither is it sufficient to satisfy our needs today. Jesus said, "I am the bread of life. Whoever comes to Me will never hunger, and whoever believes in Me will never thirst."

The Life Giver who is able to divide the marrow from the bone and who breathes life into the blood, also gives motivation and inspiration. His analysis of thoughts and intentions' fragments provides the basis for His healing and for our receiving words that are the "joy and rejoicing" of the heart. Crafted specifically for every individual, his word gives assurance of His faithfulness, His power, and His love. May His Word designed just for you be revealed to you and guide your life today and every day.

John 6:35
Jeremiah 15:16
Hebrews 4:12

"A rose by any other name would smell as sweet," Juliet says of Romeo's name. One's name really doesn't matter, she is saying. Has being in love swayed her logic? Of course, naturally speaking, many attachments come with one's surname, though the word itself may not matter. With Jesus, however, a name is important enough to be one of the seven promises to people who "overcome" the world by their faith. The person who has faith does not accept the physical world as the ultimate reality but is well aware that the physical has its roots in the spiritual. We are spiritual beings having a human experience.

What is the new name? It is the one nobody knows except the person of faith. Jesus tells John on the Isle of Patmos, "The one who is victorious I will make a pillar in the temple of My God, and he will never again leave it. Upon him I will write the name of My God, and the name of the city of My God (the new Jerusalem that comes down out of heaven from My God), and My new name." What's in a name, the name earned through unyielding faith? Salvation. Eternity. Jesus. Everything!

1 John 5:4–5
Revelation 2:17, 3:12

His Watchfulness

The towers on the two highest peaks outlining our green valley are helps in some way: one, a lookout for fires; the other, a navigation aid for airplanes. Their sturdiness and permanence are taken for granted, and local residents rarely pay attention to them, yet their value is evident. Sometimes the strong tower that is the name of our Lord is regarded similarly. Solomon says that righteous people are safe in this tower; they are those that, through faith, bear His name (Christian). Saying the word *Jesus* means acknowledging His presence and inviting the love of heaven. However, His faithfulness watches over us continually regardless of our recognition of it.

The eyes that lift to the hills know from where help comes. The "sun will not smite you by day nor the moon by night" because He towers above even the sun and moon, watching for the enemy. Like the keeper in the gate tower, He watches our "going out and our coming in," His eyes spanning the circumference for our safety. How much greater is His influence in our lives when we are aware of His keeping, when we ask in which direction the path is safe, how we might dodge or surmount the obstacles. Help has come already. We need but look to it, accept it, and receive it.

Proverbs 18:10
Psalm 121:1–8
Romans 14:11

Heaven's Joys

Has your giggle box ever gotten turned upside down and you just couldn't quit laughing? How contagious such joy is. The five joys of heaven that resound through the ages give us reason to be happy. Visualize the great sea of heaven's angels that sang and praised God when Jesus was born, when a sinner has returned to the fold, when the seals of heaven's book were opened that revealed God's purpose and plan for man, when the redeemed are gathered home and when the righteous triumph.

That the most powerful of all existence would yield in the face of damaged, imperfect man to bring him back to a state of perfection defies understanding. What joy we have when a car or four-wheeler or the air conditioning is fixed, but the Creator gave Himself, not just His talents, to fix the pottery that Satan had damaged. How we are loved! No wonder John's weeping turned to exultant joy when Jesus stepped forward to reveal His love for man, His creation. What unfathomable love he saw. Because heaven rejoices, you and I can too. Be happy today.

Luke 2:13–14, 15:7
Revelation 5:9–10, 14:2–3, 19:6

The Keeper's Peace

As jewels are found in the depths of the earth, so are treasures found in the meditations of the heart when our thoughts are on God. We learn that Christ's, the keeper's, peace dwells in beds of truth, honesty, justness, purity, loveliness, goodness, virtue, and praiseworthiness. Focus on these qualities invites the peace of God "which passes all understanding,"

Troubled? God is there. You can feel Him in your spirit and know Him in your mind. Paul learned to be content in whatever condition he found himself, whether fat or lean, rich or poor, for he knew God was his strength and He would provide for him in more meaningful and fulfilling ways than the things of earth ever could. With such confidence, we ask of the Father, simultaneously thanking Him for His provision we know will come. Such a mind-set is the precursor of peace.

Philippians 4:6–8,11, 13, 19

The Price of the Word

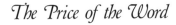

The coin in Jesus's hand is red. With it He has purchased the slave that crawls over the quarry's rocks, mangled because stones have fallen on him. He, the alpha and omega, heals the bought-back person who calls from his place of brokenness since He, the Keeper of the word, has but to speak a syllable and life is changed. Jesus, who is worthy to break the seal of heaven's registry of the redeemed, created the man and spoke words of life into him in the beginning, as He does now.

Did Jesus know the price He would pay, the price of being separated from Himself, from the Godhead, when man's life began? Yes, amazingly, He did! What love He interwove among the cells of His creation. What heartbreak to see His children broken and bleeding. Retribution spoke at Calvary, and the Savior's bones that remained in place have never failed to uphold the structure of life He created, nor will it fail through eternity. The infallible plan of salvation, the Word that was spoken from the beginning, will last, for the Keeper never fails. His heel has bruised the serpent's head and delivered us from its venomous, deathly power. We praise Jesus, who is worthy.

Genesis 3:15
John 1:1
Revelation 5:9

Home

The dogwoods on the hill grew just the right distance apart for the boards that had "treehouse" written on them. What joy was in the building of it—the planning, the nail keg raid, concocting the pulley that we used to raise the boards. As spring turned into summer, the leaves spread their greenery over our summer's refuge, the place that inhabited our every thought. Here our minds wandered through fairy tales and marvelous adventures. In such places where one's mind dwells lies the substance of dreams, love, motivation, and life.

Israel's King David made the Most High, the Lord, his habitation. Because he did so, he saw how the Lord gave His angels charge over him to lift him up and to protect him. His love and reverence invited the Lord to deliver him, to honor him, and to give him long life. We are usually most comfortable where we reside. There we are most genuine: the shoes come off; our naked feet stand on the flooring that holds us. Similarly, before God, the nature of our heart's foundation is revealed and we understand that only uncovered feet can stand on holy ground. What amazing visions may be seen as we abide there in the courts of our God!

Psalm 91:9–15, 92:13

In the gardens of God's grace, restoration abounds. The perennials that were not supposed to bloom the next year reseed and bloom again. The varied shades of yellow, red, orange, green, and violet drink the water from the soft rains, which yield to the morning sun as it shines through the mist. The Father sees you who long for such a place in the early-morning hours, you whom the famine has left thirsting for the free-flowing waters of His Spirit and hungry for the words of the Lord, you whom he has planted anew in His favor. He hears you say, "Whom have I in heaven but You? And there is none upon earth that I desire but You." Though you were not aware, He saw you when your heart was heavy, when fear had overtaken you, and when dark clouds of confusion swirled through your mind. He carried you and filled your hands when you felt you had nothing to offer. He has made "the places round about (His) hill" a blessing for you, and showers continue to fall. Are you looking toward heaven? Is there room enough in your heart for the gifts that flow through heaven's window?

Amos 8:11
Psalm 63:1, 73:25
Ezekiel 34:26
Malachi 3:10

Strength in God

All is quiet, even in the middle of the storm where God keeps you safe. You who know the one true God are at peace, for His truth has set you free from the confusion of the enemy. You know what you're doing is right, for you have heard His still, small voice, and the details are dictated by the Master of all knowledge. Assurance comes from what He has given you to know: that He lives, He is the ever-present Savior, all things work together for your good, and He is your keeper. The dangers you meet fail to daunt you because you stand on the Rock, where life cannot be taken away. Though those around you may be trembling, un-swayed by the opinions of the world, you dwell in hope and enthusiasm. Your definition of "exploit" does not jive with those of the unbeliever concerned about the physical world because yours has to do with the life that the Holy Spirit touches through you, the new understanding you gained of His Word, the message the Spirit gave you, or the miracles of life you see and experience each day. Yes, you are a "peculiar" people. How God loves you!

Daniel 11:32
Job 19:25
John 4:42
Romans 8:28
2 Corinthians 5:1
1 Peter 2:9

The Workplace

Tugboats guide the ships loaded with cargo up the river toward Savannah's harbor. Massive and heavily laden, they stir the imagination. What are they carrying, and from where did they come? One envisions workers gathering the bananas, factories lined with unfinished cars, sewers at their machines, and craftsmen carving their wares. These are people Jesus loves in places where He would have His joy to dwell. We see Him walking along the seashore attuned to the hearts of the fishermen, in government places seeing the hearts of people like Matthew, the tax collector, and among the military healing people like the Roman centurion's servant.

In stories regarding the workplace, Jesus's concern was the hearts of the workers. His lesson about wages, for example, focuses on motives. Being motivated by love and faith in the Savior gives work a different meaning, for the worker has been promoted from a servant to a friend who understands the purpose of his labor in Christ's kingdom. The beam is nailed securely because it will hold the roof over the head of Jesus's beloved; the food cooked becomes nourishment for the children of His heart; the child taught becomes God's beloved creation. How valuable is His child who takes the message of His love into the workplace.

Matthew 8:5-13, 20:1–16
Nehemiah 4:6
John 15:15

When God Speaks

The Lion of Judah roars for you. The rumbling Jonah heard in the belly of the whale pales in comparison to the rumbling of God when "joy is withered away from the sons of men." When God speaks, the righteous are not forsaken, but fire spews from His mighty mountain of truth and destroys the enemy. When an evil Rome harassed and murdered Christians, Mount Vesuvius erupted, destroying Pompeii and other Roman cities, internal corruption weakened its base, and the Parthians invaded, demolishing the empire while God held His children in His hand, loving and protecting them, for they were sealed in His eternal care. When God speaks, He pours out His Spirit, and His sons and daughters proclaim His word, see His glory, and dream of heavenly things. The weak acknowledge their strength in Him, and places of deep hurt spring into spiritual healing fountains. When God speaks, the enemy is destroyed. Jesus, the bridegroom, has gone forth from His chamber, and the bride, the church, has come out of her closet. Joy is returned to the land. When God speaks ... May you hear Him today.

Joel 1:12, 16, 2:28–29, 3:10, 18
Psalm 37:25
Revelation 7:3

Remaining—Trust

Foamy waves nibbled at his feet as he dipped his yellow bucket into the water to fill the moat. The sandcastle, replete with spires and gables, must be protected from whomever would want to enter uninvited. In this case it was his little brother whose chubby little hands did not understand the project at hand. He kept trying to get the seashells collected from the morning's exploration along the beach and hidden in the west tower. Then came the waves, closer and closer, eating away at the walls of the castle until the whole structure dissolved.

Malachi found his friends doing similar things in his pre-Jesus world. Focusing their efforts and resources upon themselves, they ignored their obligations to give their first and best to the Lord and built "castles" that withered away. However, because of His patience, God's promise, "return to me and I will return to you," resounds through the ages in the gift of our Savior. Having explored the treasures of the world, we find the Holy Spirit, the one true and genuine gift of the kingdom of God within us. In the returning we hear His voice. In the remaining we feel His constant touch. His is the castle that will never wash away from under our feet, for it is built on the solid rock. When all else fails—Jesus. When you feel empty—Jesus. The kingdom waits: "Return to me and I will return to you."

Malachi 3:3, 6–7, 9
Luke 17:21, 15:11–32
Matthew 7:24–27

Saltiness

Salt, pepper, cinnamon, and chives may be the spice of life, but chocolate sure is good. Jesus said that we are to remain spicy—that our lives are to be ever flavored so that we do not blend with the world. If flavorings blend in too much with the batter or they have aged to the point of losing their taste, they are worthless. Like adding spice, influencing others in a positive way means thinking differently and bringing out the best in others. Jesus goes on to use another analogy: a Christian is to be as a city set on a hill, one that cannot be hidden. The truth that dwells within calls to be revealed, to be spoken, and to be embraced. Motivating, healing, and fulfilling needs, Jesus's light beckons everyone to see. When we are feeling bland, bored, and common, we need only to talk to our extraordinary God who sees, laughs, works, and cares differently. We find seasoning in His Word and in His presence. When the crowds exhausted Jesus, when Satan met Him in the wilderness, as Satan does us, and when it seemed He would die as a normal man, Jesus had but to talk to the Father. Talking to the Father will add spice to our lives also. At God's table, we may ask for it as we do at our own.

Matthew 5:13

Friendships

Mama's lavender Rose of Sharon bush has grown limbs like a massive oak tree in the middle of a field, unencumbered with other trees too closely grown. The Rose of Sharon in Jesus's world was the rose of roses, the most beautiful in all the Holy Land. Solomon's love song comparing the bridegroom to the Rose of Sharon is a fit description of Jesus's love song to the church. The most beautiful of the most beautiful, Jesus's love for the sons and daughters of His church supersedes the affection in the greatest friendships, such as that of David and Jonathan, whose soul "was knit with the soul of David," or that of Naomi and Ruth, who said, "Wherever you go I will go and wherever you live, I will live." Friends who work together and speak to each other of Jesus are dear to His heart. Malachi says that a book of remembrance was written for those who had deep regard for the Lord and spoke often to each other of Him. God said, "In that day when I make up my jewels ... I will spare them." Those that believed on the day of Pentecost "were together and had all things in common" and they saw many "wonders and signs that were done by the apostles." Friends in Christ honor Him. Nurture those friendships.

1 Samuel 18:1
Ruth 1:16
Song of Solomon 1:6
Acts 2:43–44
Malachi 3:16

Keeping the Word

My earliest memory is of standing on the church bench beside my mother, going to sleep, and falling to the floor. Perhaps this experience is the reason I have such sympathy for Eutychus, who was sitting in the window listening to Paul and as midnight approached, fell out of the window, killing himself. Fortunately for him, Paul, filled with the word of God and through the power of the Holy Spirit, brought life back to him. Paul's many miracles, no doubt, caused many who were asleep spiritually to awaken, yet Jesus said those who hear the word only and because of their faith, keep it, are happier than those who seek signs and miracles.

The word of God is a life-giving force. When Ezekiel spoke the prophecies of God to the dry bones, the dry bones "heard"; breath entered them; sinews and flesh came upon them; they were covered with skin; and they lived! Even more, God put His Spirit in them and not only did they live, but they also knew He is the Lord. The word of the Lord has all power, yet it is simple faith that makes a person happy.

Acts 20:8–9
Luke 11:28
Ezekiel 37:4, 6, 14

Chosen

Promising beautiful pink blooms in the spring, the rhododendron's summer growth and new buds have overtaken the edge of my porch. I look forward to seeing them. My feeling for their uniqueness is hampered only by the fact that I don't know the plant's species name. Unlike my relationship with my plant, when God calls you, His children, to greater intimacy with Him, He has created you, examined you intently, and given you a name that describes your inner being, the true and spiritual reality of who you are. Similarly, His name, *I Am Who I Am* reveals His character, a revelation that beckons you to come closer. His name reveals that His being is of Himself (no one created Him), that He is unchangeable, which means He is faithful and true, and that you cannot comprehend Him, but only obey His word and trust His love. Your ability to call His name means that you know Him, that you know Him as Adonai, the Lord, and Elohim, the only true God. He is the one whose blessings will overtake you if you are obedient; He is the one who makes you the head and not the tail—a person with honor rather than dishonor, one who leads rather than is led, one who loans rather than borrows. Being chosen means responsibility and obedience; it means a mutual relationship where He knows you and you know Him. It means being consumed by His love, abundance, and honor.

Deuteronomy 28:2, 10, 12–13, 29:20
Exodus 3:14

Knowing God

God's beauty adorns the earth with its majestic mountains, waters that dash against the rocks, stars that twinkle and glitter as they adorn the skies, and rocks and minerals that layer its surface. Though such sights are often breathtaking, even deeper beauty lies in knowing the character of the Lord Himself. Fortunately, He progressively reveals Himself to His children. The three attributes that Jeremiah knew have continued to be revealed and manifested through the centuries. His lovingkindness has come in the form of forgiveness to nations and individuals, through the Savior's redemption and through His healing and powerful grace. His merciful judgment comes through his knowing the secret and hidden places of the heart and His discerning the truths of man's nature and thoughts. His righteousness flows from His great love and understanding. These are qualities He shares with you, His children, as you grow to be more like Him.

Hosea 6:3
Psalm 36:7
Jeremiah 9:24

He Is There

When your mother looked into your eyes for the first time, Jesus was there. When you took your first step, He was there. When you met your first-grade teacher, Jesus was there. When you hit your first home run, He was there. When you met your best friend, he was there. When you passed ninth grade English, Jesus was there. When you got promoted on your job, He was there. When you built your first house, He was there. He who knows your thoughts before you think them never leaves you, nor does He give you up or abandon you to anyone or anything, including trouble, hunger, battles, or struggles of any kind. Nothing in the past or in the future, not the demons of hell or the angels of heaven, can separate you from God's love. Even in physical death, His strong arms will carry you through the glorious places of heaven. He will not forget the covenant He made with you when you received Him as your Savior. Though you may conquer the land, the sea, and the air, He is in control. Though you may falter, fail, and give up, He is there waiting for you to cast your care upon Him. He is there brushing you off, holding you close, and giving you life. What love Jesus has for you, His child.

Romans 8:35–39
Matthew 6:8
Deuteronomy 4:31
1 Peter 5:7

Your Big Brother

As a teacher, I was often impressed by the fact that the toughest boys melted when their little brothers or sisters were around. I still picture a teenager walking up the hallway holding his little brother's hand, warmth written all over his sixteen-year-old face. Don't ignore *your* big brother. He cares about you. When you got into trouble, He took the whipping for you. Not only that, but He will let you ride in His car. His name is Jesus. Not only are you the apple of His eye, but He has also a great mind. Ralph Waldo Emerson said that foolishly doing the things others do or thinking the way others think without evaluating the ideas is the "hobgoblin of little minds." Consistency like that is certainly not Jesus. First, he recognizes liars who are fueled by the great liar of all time and who will abuse you and lead you the wrong way. They have no voice in His world. Second, he does not do things the way others do for His way of thinking is based on knowing the truth from the depths to the heights, not just from the ground level. He goes out to eat with people of a different sort; He does cool things on Sunday, like heal and feed people, and He goes off by Himself to talk to His Father. Our older Brother is different; He's tougher, smarter, more versatile, and kinder. He wants you around. How good it feels to say, "He's my Brother!"

Mark 1:27, 34–35, 2:15, 3:5
Zechariah 2:8

God's plans are for your well-being and to give you hope and a future. Though you may seem to be in a wilderness, confronted by the enemy on every hand, God has prepared your deliverance. The key is in the self-discipline of remembering who you are and remaining in that truth. When Jesus had not eaten for forty days, had endured temptation for forty days, and had been offered the devil's bread, He replied that God's bread is better and more important. When offered power from the devil, He replied that only God was worthy of being worshiped and served. When He was offered safety regardless of His feats, Jesus replied that God should not be tempted. Implicit in the devil's conversation was the attempt to get Jesus to believe that Jesus was not God and he (Satan) had more power than Jesus. However, knowing that Satan is a liar, a thief, a killer, and a destroyer, Jesus remembered who He is—God Himself. The enemy would like for you to forget who you are. What is the real question behind the challenges you face? Has the enemy been lying to you? Are you remembering that you are a child of the Most High King of heaven and earth? If the enemy would try to get God Himself to challenge His own identity, does He not do the same to you and me? The question is—who are you? What are God's plans for you? Who holds the true word, the power, and the storehouse?

Luke 4:4–13
Jeremiah 29:11
John 10:10

Hear What Jesus Is Saying

When the devil has told you that you are nothing because of what you have done, see My love for you. See My presence in you. Focus on the love, not the guilt, because I carried your guilt to the cross and nailed it there. Leave it where I put it. It is My forgiveness and love for you that rose from the grave, not your sins. You are not to live at the foot of the cross, focusing on the evil of it all, but on the resurrection. You have asked for My forgiveness, and I have given it. Peter, My disciple, denied that he even knew Me; yet when he saw Me, the risen Lord who loved and forgave him, he spread My love to family, friends, and many he had never seen before. You are like Peter. Paul killed many of My children, yet I forgave him. I took what the devil intended for evil and used Paul's gifts to enlarge My kingdom. I will do the same for you. Envision Me riding on the white horse, riding in victory. You are with me. My arms hold you tight. I will never let you go. You are secure. Now go, encourage, help, and strengthen your brothers and sisters.

Psalm 22:14, 18–19
Luke 22:32
Genesis 5:20
Colossians 2:14

With God, all things are possible, including the binding of evil. When Revelation saints ask, "How long?" the Lord replies that they should "rest" or trust God, who is pulling the details together according to His plan and who holds mercy and justice in His hands. When Jesus was in the wilderness after fasting for forty days, Satan tried to get Him to take the quick and easy way out—to command the stones to be made bread in order to quench His hunger, to worship Satan so that the kingdoms of the world would be His, to jump off the pinnacle of the temple so that He would not have the responsibilities of being in such a high place. Yet His eyes were fixed on who God is—the limitless, all-powerful God who owns everything and controls everything. He recognized that the ultimate end of temporary gratification and "fixes" lay in the limited hands of the enemy. David reminds us that God is worth the wait, for He rescues us from all sorts of maladies, including wandering with no sense of direction or purpose, being bound by addictions and faulty thinking, having physical illnesses, and being storm tossed by life's struggles. Like an athlete whose stamina carries him over the finish line, resting in patient and deliberate trust will carry us to victory.

Revelation 5:10–11
Psalm 107
Luke 4:1–13
Isaiah 40:31

God's Recompense

The joyous hope we have in Christ keeps us steady through the storms. Ever emanating from the experience of His love and the touch of heaven, hope flows in the promise that He will not forget. He will not forget the names written in the book of the faithful, and neither will He forget the love we have for Him or the work done in His name. He is just in all His ways. The biblical principle of giving love and service is voiced throughout the Bible. Solomon's advice to "cast your bread on the waters," for after many days you will find it or receive a return is restated by Jesus who said that if anyone gives a cup of water to these little ones, he will not lose his reward. Malachi shares the Lord's promise that He will open the windows of heaven when righteous tithes are brought into His storehouse. Paul said that we should not grow weary in doing well for others because in due time we will "reap a harvest." How great is our God whose recompense is bathed in mercy and grace!

Ecclesiastes 11:1
Malachi 3:10
Matthew 10:42
Hebrews 6:10
Galatians 6:9

Joy possessed the path of Jesus into the city of Jerusalem as he rode the donkey over palm leaves strewn in praise of Him. Though suffering would ensue, the time was soon near when the gates of heaven would be open to His children, who in turn would through faith open their hearts' doors to allow Him to enter. The love inherent in giving choice to man defies comprehension, yet Jesus goes even further when He tells Peter that hell itself will not prevail against the church that is built upon the truth of who Jesus is. What power Christians have through faith in Him and through calling on His name. When believers pray, the enemy, like the angry bull through the rodeo gate, springs forth, jumping and kicking, for the prayer warrior has invaded his space. Though Satan's reaction may initially seem to create a mess, the victory that led David to enter His courts with a song of praise and thanksgiving invites you and me to sing the victory song in the presence of the faithful and true King who calmly rides the white horse of purity and truth. May knowing the winner up front encourage you as you walk in the answers to your prayers of faith.

Matthew 16:18
Revelation 19:11
Psalm 22:7–10

His Mercies

Our gracious Father, who knows everything about you, who numbers the hairs on your head and knows about the one you left on your pillow when you got up today, has new mercies to bestow every morning. Every day is a new day, a new opportunity, a new time to acknowledge and bask in His presence. Every day is a day for you to be changed majorly or minutely, to see yourself and others differently, to live through new experiences, to know Him better. Every day moves you closer to God, the Great Creator who is constantly working, whose love for you never changes, whose grace gives you strength according to your needs for the day. The richness of life involves newness—new thoughts, newness in relationships, newness in vision, newness in behavior. Ethan the Ezrahite, famous in his day, proclaimed God's renewed love to every generation and that it reaches to the heavens to be showered on humankind continually. He is the never-failing God. His lovingkindness sees you today and every tiny variation in your being.

Deuteronomy 33:25
Psalm 89:1–2
Lamentations 3:22–23
Zephaniah 3:5
Luke 12:7

As with Jesus, the plans we have reflect the deeper self or picture of who we are. When Jesus planned where He and His disciples would spend the Last Supper, He already knew that the disciples He sent to prepare for it would meet a man carrying a pitcher of water. He already knew about its availability when he told them to ask, "Where is the guest chamber? Where I shall eat?" His ability to see and know the future told them, as it does you and me, who He is. As Jesus planned for Himself, He planned for His disciples and for the destiny of all who would believe through the ages.

When God speaks into our lives, the plans we so carefully laid out and intertwined with the answers to their complexities may fall apart like loose sticks in a fireplace because we forgot who we are in Christ. Isaiah warns that walking in the light of our own fires or our own plans leads to torment. Though we may be entangled in wild and twisted plans others—family, friends, employers, government—have made, the Lord has plans for our prosperity even amid struggles. He prepares a table before us "in the presence of (our) enemies." Having consulted Jesus (who makes crooked places straight) about our plans, we can have peace.

Isaiah 45:21, 50:11
Mark 14:12–16
Psalm 23:5
Jeremiah 29:11

God's Resources

God's resources extend beyond our imaginations. Noah, who had never seen it rain but only mist rising from the ground, experienced a flood, a miracle beyond anything he had ever seen. When the Israelites were starving in the wilderness, manna rained from heaven. When there was no water is the Desert of Sin, God told Moses to strike the rock at Horeb with the same staff with which he had struck the Nile. Moses did so, and the people had water to drink. How amazed God's chosen people must have been when seeing these phenomenon for the first time! Further, God did not stop sharing from his storehouse. After the rain came the rainbow, a colorful array Noah had never seen and the promise that God would never again destroy the earth by flood. After the manna stopped coming down from heaven and the water no longer came from the rock, God provided otherwise. These are assurances that God goes beyond the immediate to provide for the future. As these people saw that God not only has means of which we have no idea, we can also see from their testimonies as well as many others that God meets our needs at depths and in ways we cannot imagine. Let us trust Him today and be at peace.

Genesis 2:5–6, 6:11
Exodus 16:4, 17:1–6
Philippians 4:19

Interpretation

The thunder that accompanies those welcomed summer showers that cool the hot afternoon sometimes startle us, and the lightning flashes in the distance remind us that we need to get into a safe place. Often God speaks to us in a "still, small voice," but it is the rumblings and flashes in our lives that remind us of His presence and of our need to hear His voice. Our interpretation of His voice as He speaks from the "midst of the fire" reveals our closeness to Him. From the fire and cloud that gave the Israelites direction through the wilderness, God spoke though they waited for Moses to tell them what God had said. After Jesus's triumphal ride into Jerusalem before His crucifixion, an explanation of His purpose led to His heart's prayer, "Father, glorify Your name." The people who heard his voice were on different levels like a three-tiered wedding cake. One group interpreted the voice as being merely thunder, a product of nature; another explained it more closely as a supernatural phenomenon but one that was not for them. Jesus pointed out that it was for the group, to show them the glory of God. The living voice of the Holy Spirit who knows all things speaks specifically to us, giving us direction and hope. In this way, too, He shows us His glory.

John 12:27–30
Deuteronomy 5:2

A Day in His Courts

The mansions of the rich and famous appeal to our sense of beauty and lavish tastes. Living in one would be nice I'm sure (as long as I didn't have to do the cleaning). King David's palace must have been "something to behold"; however, it was David who said, "I had rather be a doorkeeper in the house of my God, than to dwell in the tents of wickedness" and "a day in thy courts is better than a thousand" anywhere else. Why would he feel that way? What is in God's house that is not elsewhere? Before Pentecost God's house held the holy of holies, where God met the priests. God was there. After Pentecost the Holy Spirit lives within the believer, yet the house of God is still a very special place that is dedicated and thus, belongs to Him. The significance of His "house" is emphasized by the place of His birth. Jesus was born in Bethlehem, the name meaning "house of bread." How appropriate that the Living Word, the bread of life, would be born in that place. In God's courts is truth that feeds the soul and gives life. His word spoken through those whom He has called is a priceless gift, for it gives hope, freedom from the strongholds of the world, and peace. Better a day in His courts.

Matthew 2:5
Psalm 84:10

Jewels

Can you see yourself basking in the reality of God's affection for you? John says that heaven's streets are paved with gold, that the walls of the New Jerusalem are made of jasper and the gates are made of pearl. How beautiful! Yet, what a metaphor we see, describing the extreme love our Lord has for us! Heaven's gates are the open arms of God like the Father's open arms who welcomed home his prodigal son. The walls of jasper and streets of gold are the fatted calf of God's love for His children. Every item speaks of love. No pearl compares to the beauty of acceptance into the innermost heart of the loving master whose intent is pure, whose loving hands have cleansed us with the precision and attention of the ultimate jeweler, whose grace has returned us to the fulfilled, happy state we traded for knowledge of good and evil in the garden of Eden.

Revelation 21:21
Luke 15:11–32

Did He lower His eyes when He said, "Mom, it is not time," but changed the water into wine anyway? Did His humanity cause Him to hesitate when He thought of the magnitude of the task at hand when all the world was destined to know about Him? Did His voice crack when He commanded the winds to cease over Galilee? Did His hand pause in midair as He reached to rub the mud on the blind man's eyes? Was He amazed at the power that flowed through Him when He said, "Can you see anything?" Did amazement cause Him to pause when He thought of the power that flowed through Him? If so, then are you surprised that you stand aghast by the power you have through Him? Are you astonished that He would plead for you that you might have the power of life through Him? Are you stunned when the Holy Spirit comes and you are aware that He cares deeply for you? What mystery abounds in that the ways and works of God are unsearchable, yet you have the mind of Christ! As you know, the wind blows where it pleases. You know the Holy Spirit works in mysterious ways. Though both man and God, as Jesus in His humanity prayed and trusted the Holy Spirit, you are also to trust His still, small voice. He loves you.

John 2:4, 3:8, 9:6
Mark 4:39
1 Corinthians 2:16

The angels do not serve you, God's children, with a spirit of drudgery and resentment, but with joy. As they shouted for joy when God laid the foundations of the earth, they praise God for the honor of doing His bidding, which includes "supplying your needs according to His riches in glory." Paul says that angels are "ministering spirits" sent to serve you who have accepted the Lord. The word *minister* inherently means "willingly" and implies "joyfully." *Ministry* means meeting physical needs as the seven were chosen to "wait on tables" by the disciples, but it also means meeting spiritual needs as the disciples did when teaching and applying the word of God. How glorious is God, who endows you with talents and abilities to take care of yourselves, but through prayer, the Holy Spirit, the intercession of the Son, and the grace of God, you have not only the Holy Spirit but also the care of an innumerable caravan of angels to ensure life and life more abundantly now and in the life to come. How vast are the "tools" and the power of your omniscient, omnipresent, omnipotent Father!

Acts 6:2–3
Hebrews 1:14
Psalm 103:20
Job 38:4, 7

Near Misses

One of my earliest childhood memories is of standing in the garden close to the barn and of a huge rattlesnake curled beneath a cucumber leaf. A few days before his death, my dad told the story of my running to the barn and telling him about the snake that was "just a singin'." Did God send an angel to preserve my life? In one of the three hundred times angels are mentioned in the Bible, David said that God will give His angels charge over you to protect you. Speaking of children, Jesus said that "their angels" continually see the face of God. Before Him, they receive instructions according to your exact need, for the Holy Spirit, who is with you, knows and communicates all things to the Father and the Son, who makes intercession for you. On numerous occasions, you may be aware of "near misses." You, being in His hands, need not, however, live in fear. Jesus said that your Father, who knew you before you were in your mother's womb, is pleased to give those who seek Him the love and security of the kingdom.

Psalm 91:11
Matthew 18:10
Luke 12:32

More Like Him

Jesus draws you closer so that you may be more like Him. When you are forgiving, when you share the message of salvation, when you are gracious, you are like Him. When you seek knowledge and wisdom from Him who reveals the deep and secret things and when you discern between good and evil, you are like Him. When you walk in the clarity of righteousness, you are like Him. When knowledge, good judgment, and righteousness walk through the door, atmospheres change: hate is broken, truth prevails, and correct answers are found. As you see and recognize Him in "His going forth," which "is prepared in the morning" and when His Holy Spirit comes "as the rain," you are set free to experience the joys of the kingdom. Unlike knowing the kings of the earth, knowing Him more intimately draws you closer in love and trust. In the shelter of His wings, you find life.

Hosea 6:3
Psalm 36:7
Jeremiah 9:24

Boldness

Did curiosity really kill the cat? What bravery it must take for him to put his paw forward, or is boldness his nature though he may seem hesitant, even scared? He is not unlike the young, tender sprouts that have pushed through the ground and continue to mature as God adorns them with their special characteristics according to His pleasure. As God's hand molds every cat and every plant individually so that each differs from another, so He shapes you and me. Being aware of our uniqueness may give us a nature of timidity, though the nature of life is variety and change. Paul, the apostle, encourages us to come boldly before the throne of Him who made us "fearfully" and who distinguished us so that God's glory would be evident, so that His works would incite awe of Him. Unlike God's command that the Israelites should not "go up to Mount Sinai or touch its base," Jesus's intercessory work calls us to pick up the nature of boldness and to stand in the presence of God, asking for mercy and grace to speak of Him whom we adore, who made us lovingly and wonderfully. Today we walk boldly before God and man as we are true to who we are in speech and action.

Psalm 139:14
Exodus 19:12
Hebrews 4:16

You are not alone. Before Jesus ascended into heaven, He promised that the Comforter would come. On a day of togetherness when the disciples were gathered in the Upper Room, He came to remain in the hearts of people who invite and welcome Him. The Comforter is the still, small voice that breaks the chains when the truth resounds through your spirit and sets you free. He is not the Word, for the Word is Jesus, who spoke God's truth to the enemy in the wilderness. The Comforter is the one who hears your heart's cry before you can form the words, the one whose message to the Father prompts Him to send the answer even at the "beginning" of your prayer as He did for Daniel. The Comforter is not an angel who comes afterward at the Father's bidding. Once Jesus in the garden of Gethsemane gave His fate to the Father, "Thy will be done," the angel came, "strengthening Him." As the Father sent angels to minister to Jesus after the temptation in the wilderness and in the garden, He bids his angels to assist you once you have given your concerns to Him. When your life is done, as He did for Lazarus, He will send His angels to carry you into heaven. Blessed are you whose God is the Lord. You will never be alone.

Luke 16:19–31, 4:11
Psalm 33:12
Matthew 4:11
John 14:16

Rain on Dry Ground

Summer showers on the dry earth arouse the plants' sagging leaves, and the oils exuded during dry times release their earthy smells. These are the smells of stillness and hope, of pausing and remembering that He is God who opens rivers in the bare hills and springs in desert valleys. He is God who examines what is not and sees what is. He sees bravery in the man hiding in the winepress and calls it to faith, for his services are needed to fight the enemy. He sees a multitude of offspring in the barren woman and calls them forth, for they are the children of the bride. He sees life in dead cells and arouses it, for the man's siblings are hurting. He saw the root that would grow "out of a dry ground" where faith had dissipated, called forth His birth in Bethlehem and named Him Jesus. He sees buoyancy in your spirit of loneliness, faith in your doubt, bravery in your fear, competence in your incompetence, encouragement in your disappointment, enthusiasm in your lethargy, prosperity in your poverty—and commands them to come forth. When you hear Him say, "I have found you," He means He has found the positive characteristics He created in you, the ones buried within you by earth's dry sand, and He calls forth the faith and joy that are genuinely a part of who you are. Be blessed today.

Isaiah 41:18, 53:2
Judges 6:12
John 11:1–44

The lion is a beautiful creature, though powerful and often vicious. John portrayed Jesus as the "Lion of Judah," for He is the all-powerful Savior of the world. John the Baptist, on the other hand, portrayed Him as the "Lamb of God." How can He be both? True power has the element of self-control, the ability to be large or small, the ability to call to account, or the ability to forgive. A lamb does not prey upon other animals or struggle when it is about to be slaughtered. Jesus had the power to "lay down or to pick up."

At its back is motivation. Jesus was motivated by His nature, by who He is—love. In His power, though He was the master of the universe, He came in the limited body of a man. In his power, He overcame the power of evil that confines man to a miserable state, breaking for all time the power of hate. What someone else means for harm, God means and uses for good. Love is not passive or weak but has the power of movement and the power of self-control. It is intelligent, thoughtful, caring, and selfless, acting in the best interest of the one loved. What awesome power is in the Lamb, who not only forgave but died that we might be forgiven. What power is in the ability to "go the extra mile."

Revelation 5:5
John 1:29, 10:18

The Lord reigns. He is from everlasting to everlasting. He does not falter or fail. All creation hears His voice as He calls their names. His majesty—power, dignity, beauty—clothes His being as He touches the world He has made. The sea's waves respond to His voice to shout His praises, to exalt one mightier than the sea itself. His acknowledgment stills the rushing waters, the noise of the waves, and He gives peace. The gracious God who speaks to His people never changes; his testimonies—his word, his righteousness—ever assure us of His power, of His control. The waters of His goodness flow abundantly, and He makes all things right, for He is holy, pure, and true. In His presence, light rolls forth from the darkness. He carries us on the waves of His breath, hears our prayers, and stills our hearts. He is God, now and forevermore. Praise His holy name.

Psalm 93

The Wedding

The shoulder-length veil covers her face as she walks down the aisle, her wedding garments draped in pure white lace. In the Jewish culture, the groom waits under the chuppah, a canopy or tent-like covering for the bride. Here in an elevated state of holiness, the two become one, and the veil having been pushed away, the two see each other clearly. Similarly, when Jesus, who compares Himself to the bridegroom and the church to the bride, pushes back the veil, not only does He, as always, see clearly but the members of the church see clearly also. He is the groom who has engraved your name on the palm of His hands, the one who holds your garments of faith continually before Him. He is the groom who adores the bride so much that His provision is not of the law but of grace. His bride is His friend; therefore, He shares everything He has "learned from" His Father. When the veil is pushed back to reveal the truth of God, the bride overflows with joy and healing because all deception vanishes. It is a place of unity and grace. In her enthusiasm, she remains among the wise who keep their lamps burning with the oil of the Holy Spirit, for she knows He is here. You are the bride; know that He is with you.

Matthew 25:4, 27:51
Revelation 21:2
Isaiah 49:16

Our Friend

What a wonderful friend is Christ! His is not a relationship of hidden secrets but one of transparency where He shares all truth. Learning how to respond to this level of friendship does not always seem easy. How do we hear truth that He so freely discloses, though it may be difficult to accept—through reading His word, through listening to the Holy Spirit, through circumstances, perhaps through the voice of others? The hunger to be in His presence draws us closer. We are drawn to the quiet stillness so we might talk to our friend as He was drawn to the hillsides away from the crowds to speak to the Father. His whisper says that He loves us as the Father loves Him. Though clouds and darkness may surround Him, His dwelling place is not the dark cloud of mystery but is in the light of revelation. In the quietness of our hearts, we know His love. We abide in Him.

John 15:9–15
Psalm 97:2

The Source

What is better than life itself? It is the source of life; it is what is life-giving. That source is Jesus. Jesus told the woman at the well that He would give her living water—water that gives life. Her life's circumstances did not matter anymore. Her excitement took her to the nearest city, telling people to come see the man who gave her water. She wanted to give them more than what she had. She wanted to give them the source, the well that never runs dry. In praising the Lord, David said, "Your loving kindness is better than life." The prize of Christ is Christ Himself, who is love. This is our hope, that we will be like Him, that we will have love that thinks beyond oneself. "Delight yourself in the Lord and He will give you the desires of your heart," David wrote. When you are close to the Lord, the desires of your heart are motivated by love, by purity of heart, by the life-giving water. Today, let us bathe freely.

Psalm 73:25, 37:4, 63:3
John 4

The Answer

What is it about fishing? Have you ever felt like a little molly craw bottom scavenging on the bottom of the creek but wanted to be a big, beautiful rainbow trout jumping gleefully in rushing white water as it clears the rocks and soars over the falls? Perhaps the disciples felt that way after Jesus had been crucified. They believed that they would be part of a fabulous earthly kingdom, but their hero had been crucified. Like the doors that the disciples hid behind for fear of the Jews, their hearts' doors had closed for lack of faith. Are you disappointed? Disillusioned? Hiding for fear of what waits? Where is Jesus? Is He not already inside your heart's door, since the kingdom of God is within you, the saved, the redeemed? Go "fishing inside yourself." Listen for His sweet voice of assurance and hope. He is already there living within you.

John 20:19, 26
Acts 2: 2,4

Printed in the United States
By Bookmasters